Pornography

Op]

Vie

SEP   1996

Other Books of Related Interest

Opposing Viewpoints Series

American Values
America's Children
America's Victims
Censorship
Child Abuse
Civil Liberties
Culture Wars
Feminism
Homosexuality
Human Sexuality
Male/Female Roles
Mass Media
Sexual Values
Teenage Sexuality
Violence

Current Controveries Series

Ethics
Family Violence
Free Speech
The Information Highway
Sexual Harassment
Violence Against Women
Violence in the Media

At Issue Series

Domestic Violence
What Is Sexual Harassment?

Pornography

Opposing
Viewpoints®

David Bender & Bruno Leone, *Series Editors*

Carol Wekesser, *Book Editor*

OPPOSING
VIEWPOINTS®
SERIES

Greenhaven Press, Inc., San Diego, CA

Photo credit: Craig McClain

Greenhaven Press, Inc.
PO Box 289009
San Diego, CA 92198-9009

Library of Congress Cataloging-in-Publication Data

Pornography : opposing viewpoints / Carol Wekesser, book editor.
    p.   cm. — (Opposing viewpoints series)
  Includes bibliographical references and index.
  ISBN 1-56510-518-4 (lib. bdg. : alk. paper)—
ISBN 1-56510-517-6 (pbk. : alk. paper)
  1. Pornography. I. Wekesser, Carol, 1963–   . II. Series:
Opposing viewpoints series (Unnumbered)
HQ471.P64619   1997
363.4'7—dc20   96-28268
                                      CIP

"Congress shall make no law . . .
abridging the freedom of speech,
or of the press."

First Amendment to the U.S. Constitution

The basic foundation of our democracy is the First Amendment
guarantee of freedom of expression. The Opposing Viewpoints
Series is dedicated to the concept of this basic freedom and the
idea that it is more important to practice it than to enshrine it.

Contents

Why Consider Opposing Viewpoints?

"The only way in which a human being can make some approach to knowing the whole of a subject is by hearing what can be said about it by persons of every variety of opinion and studying all modes in which it can be looked at by every character of mind. No wise man ever acquired his wisdom in any mode but this."

John Stuart Mill

In our media-intensive culture it is not difficult to find differing opinions. Thousands of newspapers and magazines and dozens of radio and television talk shows resound with differing points of view. The difficulty lies in deciding which opinion to agree with and which "experts" seem the most credible. The more inundated we become with differing opinions and claims, the more essential it is to hone critical reading and thinking skills to evaluate these ideas. Opposing Viewpoints books address this problem directly by presenting stimulating debates that can be used to enhance and teach these skills. The varied opinions contained in each book examine many different aspects of a single issue. While examining these conveniently edited opposing views, readers can develop critical thinking skills such as the ability to compare and contrast authors' credibility, facts, argumentation styles, use of persuasive techniques, and other stylistic tools. In short, the Opposing Viewpoints Series is an ideal way to attain the higher-level thinking and reading skills so essential in a culture of diverse and contradictory opinions.

In addition to providing a tool for critical thinking, Opposing Viewpoints books challenge readers to question their own strongly held opinions and assumptions. Most people form their opinions on the basis of upbringing, peer pressure, and personal, cultural, or professional bias. By reading carefully balanced opposing views, readers must directly confront new ideas as well as the opinions of those with whom they disagree. This is not to simplistically argue that everyone who reads opposing views will—or should—change his or her opinion. Instead, the series enhances readers' depth of understanding of their own views by encouraging confrontation with opposing ideas. Careful examination of others' views can lead to the readers' understanding of the logical inconsistencies in their own opinions, perspective on why they hold an opinion, and the consideration of the possibility that their opinion requires further evaluation.

Evaluating Other Opinions

To ensure that this type of examination occurs, Opposing Viewpoints books present all types of opinions. Prominent spokespeople on different sides of each issue as well as well-known professionals from many disciplines challenge the reader. An additional goal of the series is to provide a forum for other, less known, or even unpopular viewpoints. The opinion of an ordinary person who has had to make the decision to cut off life support from a terminally ill relative, for example, may be just as valuable and provide just as much insight as a medical ethicist's professional opinion. The editors have two additional purposes in including these less known views. One, the editors encourage readers to respect others' opinions—even when not enhanced by professional credibility. It is only by reading or listening to and objectively evaluating others' ideas that one can determine whether they are worthy of consideration. Two, the inclusion of such viewpoints encourages the important critical thinking skill of objectively evaluating an author's credentials and bias. This evaluation will illuminate an author's reasons for taking a particular stance on an issue and will aid in readers' evaluation of the author's ideas.

As series editors of the Opposing Viewpoints Series, it is our hope that these books will give readers a deeper understanding of the issues debated and an appreciation of the complexity of even seemingly simple issues when good and honest people disagree. This awareness is particularly important in a democratic society such as ours in which people enter into public debate to determine the common good. Those with whom one disagrees should not be regarded as enemies but rather as people whose views deserve careful examination and may shed light on one's own.

Thomas Jefferson once said that "difference of opinion leads to inquiry, and inquiry to truth." Jefferson, a broadly educated man, argued that "if a nation expects to be ignorant and free . . . it expects what never was and never will be." As individuals and as a nation, it is imperative that we consider the opinions of others and examine them with skill and discernment. The Opposing Viewpoints Series is intended to help readers achieve this goal.

David L. Bender & Bruno Leone,
Series Editors

Introduction

"I shall not today attempt further to define [obscenity]; and perhaps I could never succeed in intelligibly doing so. But I know it when I see it."

—*former U.S. Supreme Court justice Potter Stewart*

The vast majority of Americans oppose censorship. In most people's minds, the word itself conjures up visions of hysterical crowds throwing books on bonfires. Censorship seems anti-American and contrary to the right of free speech expressed in the U.S. Constitution's First Amendment. But many of these same Americans, upon viewing hard-core pornography or learning of a sexually violent crime in which the perpetrator copied actions seen in pornography, might argue that such pornography should be censored. The crux of the dilemma presented by pornography is this: how to balance the right to free speech against the need to protect society from potential harm.

Many people object to pornography, for a number of reasons. Some religious Americans think pornography is immoral and that it corrupts and trivializes sex, an act they believe is intended by God to be sacred. In addition, these and other opponents see pornography as potentially harmful—to its consumers, to women, to children, and to society in general. For example, some feminists oppose pornography because they believe it demeans women and incites sexual violence. Victor Cline, a clinical psychologist and University of Utah psychology professor, describes pornography as "male entertainment [that] promotes the victimization of women."

Some opponents of pornography favor imposing regulations on pornographic materials. Under current law, the production and distribution of child pornography is a federal crime. In addition, hard-core pornography deemed "obscene" is banned by various local, state, and federal statutes. According to a landmark 1973 U.S. Supreme Court case, *Miller v. California*, to be considered obscene a work must meet the following criteria:

- The average person, applying contemporary community standards, would find that the work, taken as a whole, appeals to the prurient interest.

- The work depicts or describes in a patently offensive way, as measured by contemporary community standards, sexual conduct specifically defined by the applicable law.

- A reasonable person would find that the work, taken as a whole, lacks serious literary, artistic, political, and scientific value.

Opponents of pornography advocate creating new laws and enforcing existing laws based on these standards to shield society—especially women and children—from the harmful effects of pornography. These critics insist that anti-pornography laws pose no threat to the public's right to free speech; works that conform to the Court's definition of obscenity are illegal, they maintain, and therefore are not protected by the First Amendment.

While a general consensus exists that some types of pornography—such as child pornography—should be banned, many commentators oppose the regulation of less blatantly abusive kinds of pornography. They argue that the obscenity criteria established in the *Miller* case are too subjective. For example, who is the *average* person? What precisely are the *contemporary community standards*? And what exactly qualifies as *patently offensive*? In short, opponents argue that this language allows prosecutors, the courts, and government officials to impose their own moral standards on the rest of society.

Besides pointing out the subjective nature of obscenity standards, critics pose various arguments against anti-pornography laws. Some people defend pornography as a harmless expression of human sexuality. They contend that pornography simply depicts human behavior and that neither the act of sex nor the act of viewing sex is immoral. In addition, numerous commentators—including many who disapprove of pornography—argue that anti-pornography laws are a form of censorship that, if left unchecked, will lead to a gradual, ongoing erosion of First Amendment rights. One opponent of censorship, feminist and author Leanne Katz, writes that anti-pornography laws will result in "the demonizing, eventually, of art and information and entertainment. Restrictions on sexually related materials invariably affect all those other things."

Many Americans agree with Katz that censorship is harmful. But they might also agree with Victor Cline that pornography is potentially destructive. This is the problem presented by pornography: Its value to society seems negligible and it may incite sexual violence, but censoring it might erode the right to free speech. Wray Herbert writes in *U.S. News & World Report* that the debate over pornography is one aspect of America's strident cultural war: "As is often the case with cultural skirmishes, it pits one set of good intentions against another. It also is about divisions—perhaps irreconcilable divisions—over what's decent and what's not, and how much tolerance and compromise are possible when values and rights conflict."

The cultural and social divisions that underlie the debate over pornography are among the issues examined in *Pornography: Opposing Viewpoints*. The book contains the following chapters: Is Pornography Harmful? Should Pornography Be Censored? Should Pornography on the Internet Be Regulated? What Stance Should Feminists Take on Pornography? The aim of this anthology is to help readers understand why pornography is a controversial issue and to offer insight into the views of those who oppose pornography as well as those who protest its censorship.

Is Pornography Harmful?

Pornography

Chapter Preface

Americans have a wide range of views on what should be done about pornography: some want to ban all of it, some want to regulate it, and some want to promote it. These diverse views exist primarily because people disagree about the effects pornography has on individuals and on society. If pornography is harmful—if it causes people to commit sexually violent acts, for example—then it probably should be regulated in some way. But if it is not harmful, and if it is even beneficial, then there is no need to regulate it, and harm could come from censoring it. The difficulty is in determining how pornography affects individuals and society.

Anti-pornography experts believe that pornography causes people to view others as sexual objects. This leads to a variety of harmful behaviors, they argue, from sexual harassment to violent sex crimes. These experts often cite convincing anecdotes to prove their point. For example, in a 1989 interview serial killer Ted Bundy pointed to his obsession with pornography as the key to his sexually violent behavior: "You keep craving something which is harder, harder . . . until you reach the point where the pornography only goes so far." Bundy said he saw pornography as "an indispensable link in the chain of behavior, the chain of events that led to the behavior, to the assaults, to the murders."

The aberrant acts of a few individuals such as Bundy, however, are not proof that pornography is harmful. Millions of people view pornography; the vast majority of these people do not commit violent sex crimes. In addition, those who oppose censoring pornography argue that countries such as Denmark and Japan, where pornography is unregulated and popular, have low rates of sexual violence. In contrast, in Islamic countries, where pornography is banned or suppressed, rates of abuse and violence against women are high. These facts seem to suggest that censorship, not pornography, is what is truly harmful, some argue.

As long as the evidence on pornography's effects is contradictory, the controversy concerning whether it is harmful will continue. The authors in the following chapter debate whether pornography is distasteful, disturbing, and degrading, or whether it helps people understand and explore their own sexuality in positive ways.

"Pornography, like the larva of a clothes moth, is eating away at the fabric of our nation."

Pornography Harms Society

Rosaline Bush

Pornography dehumanizes both those who view it and those who participate in its production, Rosaline Bush maintains in the following viewpoint. In addition, Bush contends, pornography promotes sexual aggression against women and children and has many other harmful effects on society. Bush is the editor of *Family Voice*, a monthly publication of Concerned Women for America, a politically and socially conservative organization that opposes pornography.

As you read, consider the following questions:

1. In what way is pornography like the Sirens' song, according to Bush?
2. What are the five most common myths about pornography, according to H. Robert Showers, cited by the author?
3. What are some of the many types of pornography cited by the author?

From Rosaline Bush, "Pornography: The Lust Connection," *Family Voice*, August 1994. Reprinted with permission from Concerned Women for America.

The *Odyssey*, written by Homer over three thousand years ago, chronicles the adventures of Odysseus after the Trojan War. On one occasion, Odysseus discovered that he and his crew would be forced to sail near the island of the Sirens. The Sirens were sea nymphs who tempted sailors with songs so captivating that any man hearing them forgot his wife, children, and home—everything that he held dear.

The seductive sirens lured men to their island with tempting promises. As the men jumped overboard, their ships crashed on the shoals, splintering into pieces. Broken bodies were strewn across the rocks as reminders of the price paid for yielding to the song of the Sirens.

Pornography is the siren song of the 90s. Its lyrics promise forbidden love, hidden knowledge of sexuality, and unimagined ecstasy. Its melodies create an insatiable appetite for more, as pornography lures its users closer to disaster. Finally, men, women and children involved in pornography end up shipwrecked with broken relationships and broken lives.

Homer's hero Odysseus found a way to avoid the seduction of the Sirens by ordering his crew to plug their ears with wax to stifle the alluring songs. Then Odysseus had himself tied to the ship's mast so that he could hear the voices, but not heed their call.

Odysseus would have a more difficult time avoiding the Sirens today, for pornography is not confined to one place. We are bombarded from every direction—advertisements, music, TV, magazines, movies, video games, telephone, and computer bulletin boards. And for those already hooked on pornography, a smorgasbord of material awaits. Peep shows, child pornography, catalogs of "sex toys" and materials designed to appeal to specific sexual interests, such as sadomasochism and bestiality, are available in this high-tech business.

It's a Myth!

Although Odysseus and the Sirens are recognized as part of Greek mythology, few people are aware that there are numerous myths surrounding pornography. According to H. Robert Showers, former deputy assistant U.S. attorney general, five of the most common myths are:

• *Pornography is protected under the First Amendment.* The First Amendment was not meant to protect libelous statements, false advertising, slander or obscene material.

• *Pornography is a victimless crime.* Women and children exploited by pornography, as well as the user, are all victims.

• *Legalized pornography will cause interest to diminish.* Like drug use, indulgence in pornography leads to greater indulgence.

• *Pornography is harmless entertainment.* Any entertainment that exploits people, driving them to promiscuous or violent behavior, is not harmless.

• *Nothing can be done about it.* Citizens can always do something.

Effects of Porn

In *The Case Against Pornography*, Donald E. Wildmon of the American Family Association (AFA) states that pornography:

• Causes and sustains sexual interest
• Provides fantasy material which often is acted out in real life
• Dehumanizes and debases women and reduces sex to a product
• Desensitizes the observer to aggression against women and children
• Teaches that pain and humiliation are "fun" for women
• Causes men to be less inhibited in committing rape
• Acts as a sex manual for consumers

Clinical psychologist Dr. Victor Cline reported after treating numerous sex offenders that even soft-core pornography without violence has "the potential of having negative effects on many viewers . . . modeling unhealthy sex-role behavior or giving misinformation about human sexuality."

Addiction—a Sad Reality

There are no harmless addictions. And nobody sets out to get hooked on pornography. But every addiction demands a first step, a first taste, a first glance, a first sip. Each successive step becomes a little easier until the person is hopelessly hooked. Most people never realize they have an addiction until it's too late. The Sirens' song has lured them over the edge where there is no turning back—and addiction has become a reality.

Dr. Cline, whose specialty is the treatment of sexual deviancy, believes that the four progressive effects of pornography are:

addiction—the need to view the material leads to a loss of free control over behavior

escalation—leads the person into progressively harder pornography

desensitization—user views others as objects

acting out—fantasizing likely becomes overt behavior

The National Council on Sexual Addiction describes sexual addiction this way: "The sexual addict is unable to control his or her sexual behavior and lives with constant pain, alienation, and fear of discovery. The addiction progresses until sex becomes more important than family, friends, or work."

The use of pornography by its very nature isolates individuals—making them more intent on satisfying selfish needs. But the business of pornography is another story. Many otherwise legitimate businesses, such as the telephone company, have become linked to pornography. Following are some ways pornography has gradually infiltrated other areas of your daily life.

TV—Your First Introduction to Porn

Television, perhaps more than any other medium, is the average person's first glimpse at pornography. It invades your home through regular programming, Home Box Office, cable—and videos. Unscrupulous Hollywood producers wield a heavy hand over both the motion picture and television industries. They determine not only who will invade your home via TV, but the manner and time of the invasion.

By far *NYPD Blue* has been the most controversial series produced in recent seasons. Described as a "moral sinkhole" by clerics across the nation, *NYPD Blue* has broken every barrier against nudity and profanity. Billed as TV's first R-rated series, the show has offered nude scenes, and a plethora of expletives and immoral characters. The show is a ratings success, but many sponsors have avoided it.

You Can Fight Porn

- Become knowledgeable about the issues concerning pornography
- Call and write law enforcement officials
- Write and call city or county government elected officials
- Write your governor and state legislators, asking for stronger state anti-obscenity laws
- Write the President, attorney general, your congressman and senator asking them to strengthen federal laws
- Write representatives of the news media and "letters to the editor"
- Initiate a petition to public officials stating your concerns
- Contact neighborhood stores that display and sell pornography
- Contact N-CAP for names and addresses of organizations that may help you
- Join with others in the fight and be persistent!

Source: National Coalition Against Pornography (N-CAP), August 1994.

Our children's minds have become the receptacles for this trash and programs like it. They have become desensitized to homosexuality, extramarital affairs, illegitimacy, profanity, and the demeaning of the family through programs like *Roseanne*, *The Simpsons*, *Married . . . With Children*, *Other Mothers* (an afterschool special), and *L.A. Law*. And we haven't mentioned the soap operas that invade the airways in the afternoon with their continual pornographic fare.

People at home during the day (including children) can hear what everybody has to say about *anything* on *Donahue* or *Oprah*.

These daytime talk shows are desensitizing audiences, says Penn State University sociologist Vicki Abt. Based on conclusions drawn from a study of 60 episodes of top-rated talk shows, Abt believes that topics like the grandmother who slept with the paperboy and the man who had sex with his mother-in-law—once considered taboo—are now treated as everyday occurrences. "Television," she says, "emphasizes the deviant so that it becomes normal."

And nowhere has the deviant become more normal than on MTV. Time, space and decency do not permit us to describe the obscene videos aired daily on MTV. Madonna, with her outrageously indecent costumes, gyrations, and perverse lyrics, has been responsible for more than her share of sexual corruption. And unfortunately, she has plenty of company. Rock bands, such as Red Hot Chili Peppers, Guns-n-Roses, and the Jerky Boys are especially obscene. With a flip of the dial, average viewers (and their children) can plummet to the lowest depths of MTV vulgarity.

Dial-a-Porn—The Link to Your Phone

Your telephone has also become a vehicle for pornography through the infamous 900 numbers. Business was so good for these pay-per-call services in 1991 that sales reached a record $975 million. Dial-a-Porn flourished as teens and children joined adults in instant phone sex.

Outraged parents demanded blocker devices to prevent minors from using Dial-A-Porn. As a result, 900 number billing plummeted to $540 million in 1993. But in November 1993, the Federal Trade Commission and the Federal Communications Commission decided to charge for some 800 numbers. Now many of the services that use 900 numbers are switching to the cheaper 800 numbers in the hope that blocker devices won't work on the 800 pay-per-call services. Once again listeners may get hooked over the phone through "auditory" pornography.

Just Listen to the Porn

Auditory pornography has taken another profitable turn in the past few years with gangsta rap. Although you may not recognize the term "gangsta rap," more than likely you have heard its reverberating beat on someone's car radio.

Gangsta rap glamorizes brutality, murder, torture, rape, dismemberment and perversion—usually directed at women. The lyrics are obscene, and the tape and compact disc covers provide "entertainment" for even a hard-core pornographer. Easily available and widely distributed, gangsta rap is especially harmful to young people who look up to rappers as heroes.

Because record companies endorse them, rappers feel their actions are validated. At least three of these infamous rappers have been arrested for violent crimes: Tupac Shakur (shooting), Flavor Flav (shooting), and Snoop Doggy Dogg (murder).

The Top Three

While rap groups are assaulting our ears, the print media is seductively plying their trade with high-tech visual images. The three most well known pornographic magazines are *Playboy*, *Hustler* and *Penthouse*. Of the three, *Playboy* employs an approach in which centerfolds are portrayed as the girl next door. So readers are deceived into believing that "everybody's doing it." For that reason, *Playboy* may be more harmful than hardcore pornography, especially to the young. *Playboy*'s articles about famous people, such as Jimmy Carter and Norman Mailer, somehow "legitimize" the pornography inside.

For years, Dwaine Tinsley created "Chester the Molester" cartoons for *Hustler*. "Chester" described every perversion from bestiality to incest under the guise of social commentary. But Tinsley was arrested and found guilty of molesting his young daughter. She had been victimized from the age of eight to thirteen. Finally Tinsley admitted, "You can't write about this stuff all the time if you don't experience it." Will we ever know how many other people were driven to incest or other perversions by Chester's "cute" antics?

Just one issue of *Penthouse*, said Judith Reisman, author of *Softporn Plays Hardball*, advertised "bestiality films, pseudo-child pornography, sadistic sex, boys with men, [and] women with dogs, cats, gorillas and pigs."

Although packaged as social commentary, art, literature, or humor, these magazines and others like them are still smut—burning powerful visual images into readers' minds.

Ultimate Ad Campaigns

Other powerful visual images appear as advertisements. And it's impossible to get away from them. If you watch TV, ride a bus, or read magazines, you have witnessed the lengths that companies will go to sell a product or an idea. The Design Industries Foundation for AIDS (DIFFA) plans to plaster cities from New York to Los Angeles with posters depicting "couples of all persuasions engaged in acts of all descriptions." Each bears the legend "Safer Sex Is Hot Sex." Yet DIFFA describes the message as "soft and romantic."

In 1988, Calvin Klein was quoted in *Vogue* magazine as saying, "I've done everything [in my ads] I could do in a provocative sense without being arrested." In June 1994, syndicated columnist John Leo said that "sexualizing children may be the final frontier" for Klein. He supported his theory in an article describing Kate Moss, one of Klein's favorite models.

Moss, who is 20 and looks 12, is the "emaciated supermodel whose vacant stare, unsmiling lips and frequently nude 105-pound body are on endless public display . . . mostly in Calvin Klein ads." Moss's photos, according to Leo, suggest a "vulnerable and compliant child, stripped for sexual use." Her photos flirt with themes of masturbation, bestiality, incest and violence. "One Obsession ad shows her bare-breasted, with blackened or bruised eyes, holding her hand over her mouth and looking upset." This Kleinography has appeared on buses and billboards where it cannot be ignored.

Child Porn—Hidden Victims

The Kate Moss brand of pornography is pseudo-child pornography. Giving the illusion of an innocent child, these pseudo-children whet the appetites of pedophiles who then prey on real children. Molesters often use pornography to seduce children into engaging in sexual activity. Victims may perceive the activity as "fun," or see it as a type of peer pressure if other "children" are involved; they may also believe an adult because he or she is an authority figure. According to a study done in 1991 by the Los Angeles Police Department, pornography was used in two-thirds of the child molestation cases over a 10-year period.

In late June 1994 the Justice Department disclosed a study it had conducted in 11 states and the District of Columbia. The department found that 10,000 female children under age 18 were raped in 1992. At least 3,800 were girls under 12. Twenty percent were raped by their fathers, 26 percent by other relatives, and 50 percent by friends and associates. Only 4 percent were attacked by strangers. The extent of rape has been difficult to document largely because of a lack of records. Many rapes go unreported since they involve family or friends.

Another Justice Department statistic states that one in three girls and one in five boys will be sexually molested before the age of 18. And according to the Attorney General's 1986 Commission on Pornography, "The sexual exploitation of children is the basis for the production and distribution of child pornography."

Pedophiles form networks in which to "trade, exchange, and traffic" child pornography—and children. These networks, which usually begin on a local level, often extend across the world. "The U.S. is the largest consumer of internationally produced child pornography," the commission found.

One of the groups operating on a national scale, the North

American Man Boy Love Association (NAMBLA), consistently pushes for lowering the age of consent for minors—claiming that children have a "right" to enjoy sex at any age.

London, Ontario, has been hailed as the "kiddie-porn capital" of Canada. Reuters News Agency reported in June 1994 that 30 men were charged with more than 1,300 counts of sexual crimes against 50 boys. The pedophiles included social workers, school teachers and a politician. Some of the victims were as young as 8 years old. Police confiscated more than 1,200 homemade videos and hundreds of Polaroid photos and child-porn magazines.

Practical Ways to Gain Freedom
from Addiction to Pornography

• Find a Christian counselor with experience in dealing with addictive behavior.

• Rid your house, car, office, etc., of pornographic books, magazines, and materials; cancel subscriptions.

• Cancel HBO, Playboy Channel, etc.; stay away from R-rated and X-rated movies.

• Spend more time with your family and less time alone; develop a wholesome hobby.

• Stay away from old friends—and places—that encourage your addiction.

Rosaline Bush, *Family Voice*, August 1994.

The report says the children caught up in this exploitation are often street kids or from troubled families. Contrary to what most people believe, these kids are not hauled off and assaulted. Instead, pedophiles entice them with promises of cigarettes, alcohol, drugs, cash or a chance to watch television. Once seduced, these children are then passed around within the pedophile ring. But when they reach 13 or 14, they are thrown back out on the street where they often turn to prostitution and crime.

How many runaways and missing children have been victimized by child pornographers? How many have disappeared into an underground labyrinth to grind out pornographic films for smut peddlers? Yet every picture of a naked child—every picture of a child coerced into performing sex with other children, adults, or even animals, is a real person—vulnerable and innocent—who is being exploited. Their childhood has been destroyed by the perverted things they have been forced to do. Those who survive are emotionally crippled, often ending up as drug addicts or suicidal—and more often than not—child abusers.

"The entire issue of pornography is a national tragedy," says Concerned Women of America president Beverly LaHaye. "And when you realize that America's children—our greatest treasure—are abused by this horrible industry, it's an outrage. When is this country going to learn that pornography in any form is harmful?" In our sophistication, have we made these victims someone else's problem? Have we become desensitized to the plight of innocent children?

That's Art?

It is evident that we as a nation are not concerned that our children and general population are being corrupted by pornography. In fact, it appears that the federal government is assisting in this corruption by using our tax dollars. The National Endowment for the Arts (NEA) was established in 1965 with an initial budget of $2.5 million. In 1994 it was $174.6 million.

Holly Hughes, who received $9375 for covering her body with chocolate and bean sprouts, filed a lawsuit against NEA when her "work" was turned down. Franklin Furnace Archive's sexually explicit video, also turned down previously, received $25,000 in 1994.

In March 1994 we paid for an outrageous performance by artist Ron Athey. After piercing his body with needles, the HIV-positive Athey cut a design in the back of his assistant. After blotting the blood, he reeled out the bloody paper towels over the audience, who panicked. NEA chairwoman Jane Alexander, defending Athey's artistic freedom, denied a cause for alarm. . . .

The NEA's cries of censorship cannot shout down several persistent questions arising from the moral "minority": Should the government fund the arts with our taxes? Where is the accountability of the recipients? How much has our culture been demeaned by the NEA's flagrant display of pornography? And most importantly—what are we going to do about it?

Porn's Link to Sexual Violence

If something is not done—and quickly—America will be steeped in more crime than it already is. There is a definite link between a pervasive pornographic attitude and sexual violence. According to Sen. Strom Thurmond (R-SC), a 1988 study by the Federal Bureau of Investigation found that a startling 81 percent of violent sexual offenders regularly read or viewed violent pornography. A Michigan State Police study found that porn was viewed just before or during 41 percent of 48,000 sexual crimes committed over 20 years. "Violent pornography is like a how-to manual for rapists and child abusers," the study concluded. And an FBI study on serial homicide concluded that the most common interest among serial killers is pornography. Serial killer Ted Bundy certainly vouched for that.

On January 23,1989, Dr. James Dobson of Focus on the Family had an exclusive interview with Bundy, who was to be executed the next day. Dr. Dobson learned that Bundy was born into a "fine, solid Christian home." But then twelve-year-old Ted discovered pornography at a neighborhood store.

As time went on, his fascination with soft-core pornography grew into an addiction. "You keep craving something which is harder, harder . . . until you reach the point where the pornography only goes so far." He saw pornography as "an indispensable link in the chain of behavior, the chain of events that led to the behavior, to the assaults, to the murders."

"I've lived in prison for a long time now," said Bundy, "and I've met a lot of men who were motivated to commit violence just like me. And without exception, every one of them was deeply involved in pornography."

Porn's Link to Organized Crime

If criminal types are involved in pornography, then a link to organized crime can be assumed. In fact, pornography is one of the largest money makers for organized crime, ranking third behind gambling and narcotics. A former FBI agent reported to the Attorney General's Commission on Pornography, "It is practically impossible to be in the retail end of the pornography industry today without dealing in some fashion with organized crime."

The commission's report added, "There seems to be strong evidence that significant portions of the pornography magazine industry, the peep-show industry, and the pornographic film industry are either directly operated or closely controlled by La Cosa Nostra members or very close associates."

Although organized crime "does not physically oversee the day-to-day workings of the majority of pornography business in the U.S., . . . they have 'agreements' with pornographers allowing them to operate businesses in certain geographical areas" (for a price). And money is the main attraction for organized crime's involvement in pornography.

Missing Link to Justice

Pornographers have enjoyed a great deal of freedom because of recent rulings in the judicial process. Many defendants plead their First Amendment rights and get off with a mere slap on the wrist.

In the past, the Supreme Court adopted a test which recognized material as obscene if to "the average person applying contemporary community standards, the dominant theme of the material taken as a whole appeals to prurient interest." With this statement, the Court defined obscenity without First Amendment protection.

But in June 1994, a federal judge in Los Angeles overturned a ban on sexually explicit magazines at county fire stations. He ruled that firefighters under the First Amendment had the right to keep pornographic magazines in their lockers, dormitories and restrooms. The ban, implemented to comply with state and federal laws concerning harassment, had been in place for two years.

Syndicated columnist Samuel Francis says that since the 1950s, the courts have generally dragged state and local legislation against pornography under the First Amendment, thereby gutting community efforts to control obscenity. Not only have laws been weakened at the state and local level, but Attorney General Janet Reno has made every effort to debilitate federal child-pornography laws.

In the case of *Knox v. the United States*, Steven A. Knox fought to have his conviction on possession of child pornography overturned. He based his defense on the fact that the young girls appearing on his videotapes were not naked. The Justice Department also argued that tapes of young girls clothed in bathing suits and panties—spreading their legs in a provocative way—were *not* pornographic.

The Justice Department had hoped to narrow and weaken the interpretation of the 1984 Child Protection Act. If it had succeeded, Knox would have gone free, and pedophiles would have rejoiced in their newfound freedom from prosecution—and the freedom to peddle their wares more openly. But the court disagreed. And on June 9, 1994, a federal appeals court in Philadelphia ruled that "the child is treated as a sexual object, and the permanent record of this embarrassing and humiliating experience produces the same detrimental effects to the mental health of the child as a nude portrayal." Therefore, the court upheld Knox's 1992 conviction. This ruling gives Americans hope that justice may still prevail. . . .

Our nation will stand or fall depending on its moral values. Pornography, like the larva of a clothes moth, is eating away at the fabric of our nation—unseen and generally untouched. But we have the power to bring the scourge of pornography into the light where it can be destroyed.

*"Much commercial erotica . . . contains images
and ideas that may well be seen as positive for
women and feminists."*

Pornography Can
Benefit Society

Nadine Strossen

Nadine Strossen is the president of the American Civil Liberties
Union (ACLU), a national organization that works to protect
Americans' civil rights. She is also a professor at New York Law
School and the author of *Defending Pornography*, from which the
following viewpoint is excerpted. Strossen maintains that pornography can benefit society by helping people understand and
enjoy their own sexuality. Pornography is simply sexual speech,
Strossen concludes, and as such should be protected and encouraged.

As you read, consider the following questions:

1. How does Strossen respond to the argument that
   pornography portrays women as sexually submissive?
2. According to the author, how can pornography help the
   disabled, gays, and lesbians?
3. How does pornography reflect feminist values, in Strossen's
   opinion?

From *Defending Pornography: Free Speech, Sex, and the Fight for Women's Rights* by Nadine
Strossen. Copyright ©1995 by Nadine Strossen. Reprinted by permission of Scribner, a
division of Simon & Schuster.

If pornography is part of your sexuality, then you have no right to your sexuality.

Catharine MacKinnon

I take this personally, the effort to repress material I enjoy—to tell me how wrong it is for me to enjoy it. Anti-pornography legislation is directed at me: as a user, as a writer. Catharine MacKinnon and Andrea Dworkin [noted radical feminists who oppose pornography] . . . are themselves prurient, scurrying after sex in every corner. They look down on me and shake a finger: *Bad girl. Mustn't touch.* That branch of feminism tells me my very thoughts are bad. Pornography tells me the opposite: that *none* of my thoughts are bad, that anything goes. . . . The message of pornography . . . is that our sexual selves are real.

Sallie Tisdale, Writer

Even if words and images could be interpreted literally, we would still have to reject the pornophobic feminists' [radical feminists who oppose pornography] simplistic stance that pornography conveys unrelentingly negative messages about women. Much commercial erotica depicts women in nonsubordinated roles, and contains images and ideas that may well be seen as positive for women and feminists.

Sexual Egalitarianism

Although Catharine MacKinnon has described pornography with characteristic oversimplification as "man's boot on woman's neck," in many films and photos, the shoe is, literally, on the other foot—rather, the woman's boot is on the man's neck, if not on an even more vulnerable section of his anatomy. The female dominatrix and male slave are familiar characters in sexually explicit materials. Taking issue with the antipornography feminists' views that women are never on top sexually, either in the real world or in erotic materials, Norman Mailer observed with his typical saltiness, "I've seen any number of pornographic films where you have girls sitting on guys' heads." And feminist aficionada of erotica Sallie Tisdale emphatically corroborates this perspective: "Women in modern films are often the initiators of sex; men in such films seem perfectly content for that to be so."

Many sexual materials defy traditional stereotypes of both women and pornography by depicting females as voluntarily, joyfully participating in sexual encounters with men on an equal basis. Procensorship feminists may well view a woman's apparent welcoming of sex with a man as degrading, but this is because of their negative attitudes toward women's ability to make sexual choices. Other viewers are likely to see such a scene as positive and healthy. As feminist lawyer Nan Hunter asked, "What if a woman says to a man, 'fuck me'? Is that begging, or is it demanding? Is she submitting, or is she in control?"

Men's rights activist Jack Kammer notes that "one of men's most enduring 'pornographic' fantasies is . . . about equalizing" sexual control between men and women, in a societal context in which women have often derived power from withholding sex. Accordingly, he notes:

> An archetype of male erotica is the woman who participates enthusiastically in sex, who loves male sexuality, who needs not to be cajoled, seduced or promised ulterior rewards. Erotica portraying such joyful, egalitarian sex does not demean women any more than men are denigrated by stories of women and men working cooperatively in an office where men no longer think it is their right to have women fetch them coffee. Ironically, [MacKinnon's] greatest effect may be only to enhance men's need for what she wants to suppress. The more women accept arguments about the inherent cruelty, selfishness and danger of male sexuality, the more men will need to fantasize, possibly by resorting to pornography, about women who offer egalitarian, joyful, trusting sexual companionship.

Even the Meese Commission [which was established by Ronald Reagan in 1984 to investigate whether pornography and antisocial behavior were related] acknowledged "two areas in which sexually explicit materials have been used for positive ends: the treatment of sexual dysfunctions and the diagnosis and treatment of some paraphilias." (*Webster's Third New International Dictionary* defines "paraphilia" as "a preference for or addiction to unusual sex practices.") Moreover, the Meese Commission recognized that pornography might have other beneficial effects, including providing entertainment, relieving people of the impulse to commit crimes (of course, this contradicts one of the Commission's other contentions, that pornography *causes* crime), and improving marital relations by teaching about sexual techniques.

Improving Sex Lives

Popular sex manuals such as *The Joy of Sex* have recommended erotic pictures and videos as aphrodisiacs, and experts widely believe that it can improve the sex lives of many couples. In a 1992 letter to the Senate Judiciary Committee, opposing the then-pending Pornography Victims' Compensation Act, Patti Britton, Ph.D., wrote:

> As a board-certified clinical sexologist, I can tell you that it is common knowledge in my field that sexually explicit films and videos are often recommended as a mode of treatment for couples or individuals with clinical sexual problems. Such materials are viewed by professionals as helpful, not harmful, assets in the treatment process.

Even for couples and individuals with no "clinical sexual problems," sexually explicit materials can spice up their sex lives, and hence solidify their relationships. At a conference at Columbia University, the eminent psychoanalyst Otto Kernberg said that inhibition too often

> limits a couple to conventional standards that stifle passion. Pornography, on the other hand, can stimulate an active fantasy life—can be an antidote to stifled passion. A rebellious sex life within the bounds of a couple can be the cement of marriage.

To the extent that erotic publications and videos offer an alternative sexual outlet for people who otherwise would be driven to engage in psychologically or physically risky sexual relations, they serve a positive public health function. This point was trumpeted by a banner that a Manhattan bookstore recently hung over a display of sexually oriented publications that had been threatened with censorship: "Enjoy some safe sex!" In the age of AIDS—to say nothing of the continuing rise of unwanted teenage pregnancies—sex itself is often fraught with risks. Yet sexually explicit materials *are* a safe alternative.

A Source of Pleasure

In addition, sexually explicit materials may well be the only source of sexual information or pleasure for many people who, for a host of reasons, do not have sexual contact with others— shy or inhibited people, people with mental or physical disabilities, people with emotional problems, gay people who are confused about their sexual orientation or are afraid to reveal or express it, people who are quite young or old, geographically isolated people, unattractive people. Disability rights activists protested Congress's attempt, in the mid-1980s, to prevent the Library of Congress from publishing *Playboy* in braille. Noting that this was "part of a long history of disabled people's sexual oppression," Barbara Faye Waxman, an expert in the sexual and reproductive health of disabled women, wrote, "[T]he last thing I'm going to do is call for any form of censorship that will inevitably have a backlash and reinforce the policies and practices that have kept disabled people sexually disempowered for so long."

Even for individuals who generally have sexual relations with other people, pornography may well serve as a welcome alternative stimulus and outlet in situations where that is not possible, such as when travel separates them from their partners. Many hotels all over the United States, including some of the finest, now offer sexually explicit videos for in-room viewing.

Erotic publications and videos serve an egalitarian, pluralistic function beyond providing vicarious sexual experiences. Pornography depicts an enormous range of people and sexual practices, thus helping *all* viewers to explore and affirm their own sexuality, their own sexual practices and preferences, and their potential sexual relationships with all other human beings. As Paula Webster has written, "Pornography implies that we could find all races, genders, ages, and shapes sexually interesting, if only in our minds."

The Power to Choose

I was taught to believe that all porn was violent. However, my own exploration quickly revealed that the majority of commercial porn is rather peacefully formulaic. . . . Ultimately I felt the antiporn feminists viewed women as being without sexual self-awareness. Their arguments for the elimination of porn were shaky and flawed. Their claims denied women independence by refusing to acknowledge that women had rich sexual fantasies, powerful libidos, and the power to choose.

Lisa Palac, in NEXT: *Young American Writers on the New Generation*, 1994.

This radically egalitarian premise that sex and sexual expression can break down any other barriers separating people is no doubt one of the reasons that they consistently have been viewed as threatening to established political, as well as moral and cultural, norms.

Instruction for Women's Sexual Pleasure

Contrary to the stereotypes of pornophobic feminists, many other feminists and many women in general say that porn has much to offer them. Let's now consider their views, so often drowned out by antiporn crusaders. Judith Kegan Gardiner, professor of English and Women's Studies at the University of Illinois, has cataloged some of pornography's positive aspects, specifically from a woman's perspective:

For some women, pornography may actually de-objectify women because they can use it to validate their own desires and pleasures. They can also reinterpret or take control of the fantasy. For example, they may point out that a particular pictured position is not fun, but awkward and uncomfortable. Furthermore, women too can make comparisons between their lovers and the performers, for instance to the male stars' larger organs or more sustained erections, and they can use the pornography to encourage or instruct their partners how to please them. Pornography may also serve women to defamiliarize and romanticize the relationships in which they are already. For example, in a pornography sequence produced by the women of Femme Productions, a woman dressed in sexy finery is picked up by a man on the street who turns out to be her husband. The woman has left their child with her mother in preparation for their sexy night together.

At the most basic level, porn provides information about women's bodies and techniques for facilitating female sexual pleasure, which is otherwise sadly lacking in our society. Precisely to fill this gap, a growing number of women are becoming producers, as well as consumers, of pornography. . . .

Lesbian and Gay Images and Identity

As law professor Kathleen Sullivan has written, "In a world where sodomy may still be made a crime, gay pornography is the samizdat of the oppressed." In light of the long-standing and ongoing legal and societal discrimination faced by lesbians and gay men, materials depicting and exploring their sexuality are especially important, serving to educate, liberate, and empower. The positive role that lesbian erotica played in her own life was described by the Canadian lesbian feminist writer and activist Chris Bearchell:

> My erotica "habit" began when I was coming out in a small Canadian city in the late '60s. It was hard admitting that I was sexually attracted to other women, but it got a lot easier when I saw pictures of women having sex. I squirreled away copies of soft-core men's magazines . . . I was vaguely disappointed by the lack of authenticity in much of what I saw, and by the meagerness of my collection, but I never gave up hope of finding more and better (juicier) images. Eventually, I moved to the big city—Toronto—and grew from a baby dyke into a gay activist and journalist. Then, what seemed to be a miracle happened. . . . [L]esbians began to make and distribute sexual imagery of our own.

Referring to another beneficial aspect of porn from a lesbian and gay perspective, writer Pat Califia has noted that, should the antipornography feminists have their way, "homosexuals and other sexual minorities would lose a vital source of contact—the sex ads.". . .

Fantasies for Feminists and Other Freedom Fighters

> [I]f social convention, backed by religion and law, confines sexuality to the heterosexual, monogamous, marital, familial, and reproductive, then the ambisexual, promiscuous, adulterous, selfish, and gratification-centered world of pornography is a charter of sexual revolution that is potentially liberating rather than confining for women.
>
> Kathleen Sullivan, Stanford University law professor

Several anthologies of feminist writings illuminate the range of messages in pornography, specifically from the viewpoints of feminists and women in general. Feminist writer and literature professor Ann Snitow, who coedited one such anthology, *Powers of Desire*, has described some of porn's positive facets:

> Pornography sometimes includes elements of play, as if the

fear women feel toward men had evaporated and women were relaxed and willing at last. Such a fantasy—sexual revolution as *fait accompli* . . . can . . . be wishful, eager and utopian.

Porn can depict thrilling (as opposed to threatening) danger. . . . [S]ome of its manic quality . . . seems propelled by fear and joy about breaching the always uncertain boundaries of flesh and personality. . . .

Some pornography is defiant and thumbs a nose at death, at the limitations of the body and nature. . . .

Porn offers . . . a private path to arousal, an arousal that may be all too easily routed by fear or shame. . . .

[P]ornography also flouts authority, which no doubt in part explains its appeal to young boys.

Feminist artist Myrna Kostash theorizes further positive, liberating aspects of pornography: "Until there is a revolution in the institutions that regulate sexual relations—the family, the school, the workplace—perhaps the pornographic fantasy is one of the few ways that women and men, captives together of those institutions, victims alike of their alienating procedures, are permitted connection."

Eyes Wide Open

We're just beginning to make up the rules about feminist pornography. And it seems to me there are more possibilities for changing oppressive images of women by exploring pornography with our eyes open than by forcing them shut.

Laura Fraser, *EXTRA!*, July/August 1993.

Pornography also contains many elements that are harmonious with feminist values. As the Feminist Anti-Censorship Taskforce [has] noted, it "may convey the message that sexuality need not be tied to reproduction, men or domesticity." Feminists Lisa Duggan, Nan Hunter, and Carole Vance have suggested additional profeminist aspects of pornography:

[P]ornography has served to flout conventional sexual mores, to ridicule sexual hypocrisy and to underscore the importance of sexual needs. Pornography carries many messages other than woman-hating: it advocates sexual adventure, sex outside of marriage, sex for no reason other than pleasure, casual sex, anonymous sex, group sex, voyeuristic sex, illegal sex, public sex. Some of these ideas appeal to women reading or seeing pornography, who may interpret some images as legitimating their own sense of sexual urgency or desire to be sexually aggressive. Women's experience of pornography is not as universally victimizing as the [MacKinnon-Dworkin] ordinance would have it.

Indeed, as feminist writer and video artist Sara Diamond has noted, "[F]eminism and porn have something in common. Both insist that women are sexual beings. Both have made sex an experience open to public examination and . . . debate."

In response to the charge by procensorship feminists that pornography exploits women, Ann Snitow explains that its subversive quality challenges the entire status quo, including social structures that inhibit women's freedom:

> Though pornography's critics are right—pornography *is* exploitation—it is exploitation of everything. Promiscuity by definition is a breakdown of barriers. . . .
>
> It is a fantasy of an extreme state in which all social constraints are overwhelmed by a flood of sexual energy. Think, for example, of all the pornography about servants fucking mistresses, old men fucking young girls, guardians fucking wards. Class, age, custom—all are deliciously sacrificed, dissolved by sex.

The fact that pornography always has rebelled against conventional constraints is precisely the reason it always has provoked such anxiety among moral traditionalists and political conservatives. Just as sex itself has enormous power to break down individual and social boundaries, so speech about sex threatens all manner of accepted bounds; the more unconventional the sexual expression is, the more revolutionary its social and political implications become. . . .

Just as *suppressing* sexual speech plays an essential role in *maintaining* the political, social, and economic status quo, conversely, *protecting* sexual speech plays an essential role in *challenging* the status quo. Accordingly, the women's rights cause should naturally be allied with the free speech cause for all expression, including sexual. Once again, the sexual *is* political.

*"Pornography . . . contributes to sexual violence
in a real and direct way."*

Pornography Incites
Violent Sexual Crime

Donna Rice Hughes and John D. McMickle

In the following viewpoint, Donna Rice Hughes and John D.
McMickle write that hard-core pornography often contains
scenes of rape, torture, and bestiality. They maintain that such
horrific scenes incite viewers to commit violent sexual crimes,
and they argue that pornographers should be held liable for
these crimes. Rice Hughes is director of communications for
Enough Is Enough!, a bipartisan women's group opposed to
hard-core pornography. McMickle is counsel to the U.S. Senate
Committee on the Judiciary, Subcommittee on Administrative
Oversight and the Courts.

As you read, consider the following questions:

1. Why are even the most benign forms of pornography
   harmful, according to the authors?
2. Some believe that if pornographers were held liable for
   crimes inspired by pornography, then the actual perpetrators
   would not be held responsible for their crimes. How do the
   authors refute this argument?
3. What question do the authors believe should be explored
   rather than "is pornography harmful"?

Donna Rice Hughes and John D. McMickle, "Defensive Spin by Porn's Apologists," *Washington Times*, February 1, 1995. Reprinted by permission.

Does hard-core pornography serve any beneficial purpose? The apologists for the pornography trade are suspiciously silent on this question. Much of their energy is devoted to the proposition that not all pornography causes violence and rape, but very little is said about pornography's other harmful consequences or why America is better off because of pornography. Nadine Strossen's new book, *Defending Pornography: Free Speech, Sex, and the Fight for Women's Rights*, is a case in point. Ms. Strossen's unexceptional conclusion is that some types of pornography might not be harmful.

And this, it appears, is the best that can be said for hard-core pornography. Unlike firearms, which have beneficial as well as harmful uses, pornography serves no good purpose.

Perhaps the most fundamental need of every person is to love and be loved, a desire that is easily exploited by unscrupulous profiteers. In its most benign forms, pornography creates an attitude where sex is a mere commodity and intimacy atrophies. At its worst, hard-core pornography (i.e., incest, rape, bestiality, torture and mutilation), which has never been protected by the First Amendment, contributes to sexual violence in a real and direct way.

A case in point. Thomas Schiro, who was convicted of the rape and murder of a 28-year-old woman, unsuccessfully raised the "pornography made me do it" defense. Schiro's brutal crime occurred after being thrown out of a coin-operated "peep-show" booth for exposing himself to a clerk. Shortly thereafter, Schiro raped Laura Jane Luebbehusen three times before deciding to bludgeon her to death. A forensic pathologist concluded that Schiro then raped Laura Jane's corpse and "chewed on several parts of her body." According to a psychologist who testified at trial, Schiro had been exposed to hard-core pornography depicting rape and simulated murder since he was 6 years old. Another expert testified that continual exposure to hard-core pornography creates "a person who no longer distinguishes between violence and rape, or violence and sex."

Make Producers of Porn Liable

Despite this evidence, the decision to reject the "pornography made me do it" defense was proper—Schiro should be held accountable for his violent acts. The more interesting question is whether the producers and sellers of the pornographic materials that quite obviously contributed to Laura Jane's horrible death should be held liable for inciting rape. In the view of many Americans, the answer is yes.

A few, however, including the adult entertainment industry and Ms. Strossen of the American Civil Liberties Union, assert that recognizing the obvious relationship between hard-core pornography and violence would permit rapists to go free, or at least avoid taking responsibility for their violent acts. Not so. A drunk driver who kills a pedestrian can no more use the consumption of alcohol as a legal defense than the rapist could use his consumption of hard-core pornography. And in some places, bar owners who serve liquor to patrons who later injure someone while driving drunk are held liable. There is enough blame to go around.

Reprinted by permission: Tribune Media Services.

As a matter of sound public policy, pornographers should be held accountable for the personal and social pain that are the consequences of their pornography. And Schiro's case is not unique. In 1990, for instance, a brutal genital mutilation occurred identical in detail to a mutilation described in a *Hustler* magazine article. The article described precisely how to mutilate genitalia after removing the victim's eye without severing the optic nerve so that the victim could view his own torture. Ours would be a brutish society indeed if communities could not hold accountable those who incite violent and vicious crimes. The same should be true for pornographers who peddle material that incites sexual violence.

The pornography apologists' refusal to recognize the relationship between hard-core pornography and rape is dishonest. It reveals a way of thinking that is abhorrent to our culture—that profit is more important than respect for human dignity. To avoid forthrightly addressing the relationship, the pornography apologists resort to deflection and distraction, focusing on an overly broad definition of pornography that has never been accepted in this country by the mainstream public or the courts.

A profit-driven pornography industry, with the help of smoke-and-mirror tactics, is waging war against women and the moral fabric of our society. As a result of this campaign of deception, the wrong question is being asked—is pornography destructive? Unanswered is the question: Is it constructive?

The answer is, the best case for pornography is that some pornography is less destructive, preying on our deepest needs and diminishing our capacity for intimacy. In its most destructive forms, pornography directly contributes to sexual violence. Either way, society derives no benefit from pornography.

"There is no reason to believe that pornography causes violence."

Pornography Does Not Incite Violent Sexual Crime

Wendy McElroy

Wendy McElroy is a freelance writer and the former president of Feminists for Free Expression/Canada. In the following viewpoint, excerpted from her book *XXX: A Woman's Right to Pornography*, McElroy argues that there is no evidence that pornography incites viewers to commit sexual crimes. In fact, the author contends, pornography may enable people to channel their sexual energies in harmless ways, thereby preventing acts of sexual violence.

As you read, consider the following questions:

1. How were the Meese Commission hearings biased against pro-pornography feminists, according to McElroy?
2. Why is the anti-pornography feminist view insulting to men, in the author's opinion?
3. According to McElroy, what do the rape rates in Germany and Japan suggest about the effects of pornography?

Pornography benefits women, both personally and politically.

After reading this, anti-pornography (or radical) feminists will consider me a heretic—fit only for burning. Or, to put it in more politically correct terms, I am a woman who is so psychologically damaged by patriarchy that I have fallen in love with my own oppression. My arguments will be dismissed.

In other words, if I enjoy pornography, it is not because I am a unique human being with different preferences. It is because I am psychologically ill.

Anti-pornography feminists try to silence any real discussion of pornography. Catharine MacKinnon, for example, flatly refuses to debate women on this subject. Feminists who disagree are treated as traitors. Their bottom line is: Individual women must not be allowed to question the sexual interests of women as a class.

Standing Up for Pornography

Liberal feminists often argue *against* censorship rather than *for* pornography. Many of them view censorship as being far too dangerous a solution to the "problem" of graphic sex. They believe censorship could and would be used to stifle the voices of women. Nadine Strossen's book *Defending Pornography* eloquently argues this point. In response, radical feminists consider their liberal counterparts to be the "dupes of men," or "co-conspirators in gender oppression."

Yet many liberal feminists accept the basic anti-porn assumptions of radical feminism. For example, they generally accept the idea that pornography degrades women. This agreement does not seem to create common ground, however.

Why? Because anti-porn feminists will not tolerate any attempt to apply freedom of speech to pornography. In her book *Only Words*, MacKinnon goes so far as to deny that pornography consists of words and images, both of which would be protected by the First Amendment. She considers pornography—in and of itself—to be an *act* of sexual violence.

For years, anti-porn feminists effectively silenced dissent on pornography. Here and there, a renegade like Sallie Tisdale became so fed up with being ashamed of her own sexual responses that she would admit to enjoying adult films. When Tisdale explained in *Harper's* how pornography enriched her life, her admission caused a sensation. Tisdale's latest book bears the same title as her pioneering article, *Talk Dirty to Me*. It continues her celebration of sex.

A group of hardy feminists are now standing up to defend pornography . . . as harmless, as pleasurable, as fun. . . .

One basic accusation hurled against pornography is that it causes violence against women. Radical feminists claim there is a cause-and-effect relationship between men viewing pornography and men attacking women, especially in the form of rape.

But studies and experts disagree as to whether there is any relationship between pornography and violence. Or, more broadly stated, between images and behavior. Even the pro-censorship Meese Commission Report admitted that much of the data connecting pornography to violence was unreliable.

This Commission was a national effort to define and suppress pornography. It was a circus of public hearings, conducted by the U.S. Attorney General's Commission on Pornography aka the Meese Commission. Established in May 1984, this eleven-person body received a mandate from President Ronald Reagan to investigate what he called "new evidence linking pornography to anti-social behavior." Reagan obviously wanted to overturn the findings of the 1970 Federal Commission on Pornography and Obscenity, which had been set up by then-president Richard Nixon. The earlier commission not only found no link between violence and pornography, it also urged the repeal of most obscenity laws. Its findings were dismissed.

The Meese Commission carefully avoided a repetition of this embarrassing liberalism. For example, the first Meese hearing allowed testimony from forty-two anti-porn advocates and only three pro–freedom of speech people. Many anti-censorship groups, including major writers' organizations, were denied the chance to speak. The reason given: lack of time.

But when radical feminist Dorchen Leidholt, who had already testified, rushed the microphone along with a group of other women, she was given extra time. The microphones stayed switched on. And a written copy of her remarks were requested by the chairman.

No Connection

Is it any wonder that the Meese Commission found there to be a relationship between pornography and violence? In the *Virginia Law Review*, Nadine Strossen commented on the shaky ground beneath this finding: "The Meese Commission . . . relied on Professor Murray Straus' correlational studies . . . to 'justify' their conclusions that exposure to 'pornography' leads to sexual assaults. But, as Professor Straus wrote the Commission, 'I do not believe that [my] research demonstrates that pornography causes rape.'"

Other studies, such as the one prepared by feminist Thelma McCormick (1983) for the Metropolitan Toronto Task Force on Violence Against Women, found no pattern to indicate a connection between pornography and sex crimes. Incredibly, the Task Force suppressed the study and re-assigned the project to a pro-censorship male, who returned the "correct" results. His study was published.

Moving away from studies, what of real world feedback? In West Germany, rape rates have slightly declined since 1973, when pornography became widely available; meanwhile, other violent crime has increased. In Japan, where pornography depicting violence is widely available, rape is much lower per capita than in the United States, where violence in porn is restricted.

It can be argued that all forms of violence are lower in these countries. The low rate of violence against women may be nothing more than a reflection of this. Nevertheless, if pornography *is* intimately connected to violence against women, you would expect to see that connection to be manifested in some manner. It is up to radical feminists to explain why it is not.

No Consistent Pattern

Research has shown no consistent pattern between the availability of sexual materials and the number of rapes from state to state. . . . Procensorship feminists . . . maintain that the availability and consumption of pornography, including violent pornography, have been increasing throughout the United States. At the same time, though, the rates of sex crimes have been decreasing or remaining steady. The fact that rapes . . . have not increased provokes serious questions about the procensorship feminists' theories of pornography-induced harm.

Nadine Strossen, *Defending Pornography: Free Speech, Sex, and the Fight for Women's Rights*, 1995.

But even generously granting the assumption that a correlation *does* exist between pornography and violence, what would such a correlation tell us? It would certainly not indicate a cause-and-effect relationship. It is a fallacy to assume that if A can be correlated with B, then A causes B. Such a correlation may indicate nothing more than that both are caused by another factor, C. For example, there is a high correlation between the number of doctors in a city and the number of alcoholics there. One doesn't cause the other; both statistics are proportional to the size of the city's population.

Those researchers who draw a relationship between pornography and violence tend to hold one of two contradictory views on what that connection might be. The first view is that porn is a form of catharsis. That is, the more pornography we see, the less likely we are to act out our sexual urges. The second view is that porn inspires imitation. That is, the more pornography we see, the more likely we are to imitate the sexual behavior it represents.

Researchers who favor the catharsis theory point to studies, such as the one conducted by Berl Kutchinsky, which found that an increased availability of pornography in Denmark correlated with a decrease in the sex offenses committed there.

Radical feminists advocate the imitation theory, the idea that men will try to re-create the situations they see on a screen. The first comment to make about this claim is how insulting it is to men. Radical feminists seem to believe that men are soulless lumps of plasticine on which pornographers can leave any imprint they wish.

Radical Feminists View a Lot of Porn

Although anti-porn feminists cry out against viewing pornography, they must admit that there is at least one group of people who can survive such exposure without harm—namely, themselves. In their zeal, radical feminists view more pornography than the general population. Moreover, they dwell upon the small percentage of pornography that depicts violence. Either they are wonder women or they are human beings who have a normal response to brutal pornography: They are repelled by it.

Radical feminists are well aware of how disturbing most people find brutal pornography. This is precisely the reaction they count on when they show pornographic slides and films at lectures and debates. They count on the fact that most people are revolted by graphic violence and brutality. Ironically, this revulsion has sometimes worked against the anti-porn cause. Several years ago in New York City, the group Feminists Fighting Pornography was ordered to remove a display of pornography that it had set up in Grand Central Terminal. Commuters were upset by the sight of it. The New York Civil Liberties Union successfully defended the feminists' right to display pornography.

Despite the evidence that most people are repelled by pornography that depicts violence, radical feminists parade anecdotal studies that draw the connections they desire. For example, interviews in which rapists confess they consumed violent pornography before committing their crime. Even if these stories are credible, they indicate nothing more than that men who rape may also tend to enjoy brutal images of sex. They say nothing about the reactions of men in general.

There is no reason to believe that pornography causes violence. There is a growing body of evidence that indicates that pornography either acts as a catharsis or has little impact at all.

"In 25 per cent of the cases, pornography appeared to be a significant factor in the chain of events leading to a deviant sexual act."

Studies Show That Pornography Causes Violence

Mark Nichols

Studies have revealed a causal link between pornography and sexual crimes, Mark Nichols writes in the following viewpoint. Nichols cites several studies showing that many men who committed violent sexual crimes were also addicted to pornography. Other studies, he maintains, indicate that regular viewing of violent pornography desensitizes people to violence and may lead them to view violent sexual crimes as less abhorrent. Nichols is a writer for *Maclean's*, a Canadian newsmagazine.

As you read, consider the following questions:

1. What role did pornography play in the violent crimes studied by Bill Marshall, according to Nichols?
2. What were the results of the study by Dolf Zillmann and Jennings Bryant in which male volunteers were shown explicit pornography, according to Nichols?
3. According to the author, what does Edward Donnerstein suggest as a remedy for the harmful effects of pornography?

Mark Nichols, "Viewers and Victims," *Maclean's*, October 11, 1993. Reprinted with permission.

In a pornographic film made somewhere in the United States, a man is shown performing a sexual act with a girl of about 4. Bill Marshall, a psychology professor at Queen's University in Kingston, Ontario, who has seen the movie, says that the little girl keeps looking past the camera at someone—perhaps a parent or other relative. "She is frightened," says Marshall, "and she is looking to this person for help." The ugly images reveal the effect that the experience had on the child. But what effect does such pornography have on the viewer? Marshall is convinced that in some cases pornography can play a role in sexual offences. As director of a sexual behavior clinic in Kingston between 1980 and 1985, he interviewed 120 men who had raped women or molested children. He concluded that in 25 per cent of the cases, pornography appeared to be a significant factor in the chain of events leading to a deviant sexual act. Not all people will be as dangerously affected by violent pornography or by porn involving children, adds Marshall, "but some vulnerable people will be."

In attempting to establish links between pornography and sexual offences, most other researchers do not go quite as far as Marshall. Neil Malamuth, a psychology professor at the University of Michigan in Ann Arbor, cautiously concludes that the messages contained in some types of pornography—combined with other factors, including personality type—can probably, in some cases, "contribute to antisocial behavior." And Edward Donnerstein, a psychologist who teaches at the University of California at Santa Barbara, says that violent pornography may make some people less sensitive to violence. As for sexually explicit, nonviolent images involving consenting adults, says Donnerstein, "there is absolutely no evidence that shows this stuff is harmful."

In his Kingston study, Marshall found that pornography could play a number of roles in sexual offences. In some cases, men told him that they looked at pornography with the intention only of masturbating, but then became aroused and "decided to go out and assault a woman or a child." Other offenders said that they deliberately used pornography to "prime" themselves to commit sexual assaults. Marshall believes that the men who cited pornography as playing some role in their offences "might have been looking for excuses." But "keeping that in mind," he adds, "I still think pornography was a factor in their behavior."

Education Necessary to Counteract Pornography

Other social scientists have carried out studies in which exposure to pornography appeared to make antisocial behavior seem acceptable. In a study during the early 1980s, two leading U.S. researchers, Dolf Zillmann and Jennings Bryant, subjected some male volunteers to explicit pornography that included movies in which women were depicted as sexually insatiable. Later, the volunteers were asked to suggest prison terms for a man convicted of rape. The men who had viewed the pornography were more inclined to suggest more lenient prison terms than members of a control group that had not seen the porn.

A Perfect Instruction Manual

Pornography is the perfect preparation—motivator and instruction manual in one—for sexual atrocities.

Catharine MacKinnon, *Ms.*, July/August 1993.

While researchers agree with the laws against child pornography in Canada and the United States, they differ over whether sexually violent material should be suppressed. The latter is illegal in Canada, but can still be legally obtained in the United States. According to Donnerstein, studies have shown that nonsexual materials featuring violence—many TV shows and movies fit the bill—can influence attitudes as much as violence combined with sexually explicit material. "If you start banning things," says Donnerstein, "then the problem is, where do you stop?" Instead, Donnerstein argues that society must begin offsetting the effects of mass media and pornographic violence through massive education programs starting at the grade-school level. "As educational programs take effect," adds Donnerstein, "certain kinds of images will become unacceptable, just as the racist attitudes reflected in the movies of 50 years ago are completely unacceptable today."

"The experiments that seek to prove that all men are potential rapists . . . have always troubled us. Now we know why."

Studies Showing That Pornography Causes Violence Are Flawed

Playboy

In the following viewpoint, the editors of *Playboy* criticize the accuracy of studies that show a causal connection between pornography and violence. The editors conclude that such studies are so poorly designed that the results cannot be valid or conclusive. *Playboy* is a monthly magazine that features soft-core pornography.

As you read, consider the following questions:

1. According to the editors, what is proved by the original experiment they describe?
2. Who is to blame for violent sexual crime, in the editors' opinion?
3. What do the editors mean when they say, "real men leave"?

For years social scientists have tried to gauge the effect of porn on men's behavior. You have probably read some of their conclusions in newspaper editorials or on fliers from antiporn ministers, or heard them in diatribes by feminist law professors, or in pompous speeches from politicians considering new antiporn legislation. In short, the finely hedged message seems to be that certain types of porn increase the chance of aggressive behavior toward women.

Social science in this case seems to blend seamlessly with political science. When expert testimony from social scientists favors prevailing social wisdom, it's cited and applauded. When it goes against the prevailing social consciousness, it's ignored.

The experiments that seek to prove that all men are potential rapists, beasts who can turn violent at the glimpse of a woman being treated violently, have always troubled us. Now we know why. William Fisher, a psychologist at the University of Western Ontario, reviewed a previous experiment and discovered a serious flaw.

A Bad Three-Act Play

Fisher followed the structure of the original experiment, which can be viewed as a bad three-act play.

Act one: A male college student enters a lab, where he meets a female "teacher." The student writes an essay or performs a task; the woman gives him six to nine powerful electric shocks, supposedly to help him learn. In some experiments, the woman adds insult to injury by asking derisively, "How did you ever get into this university?" or commenting within earshot, "If I had to choose between a bed of nails and this guy, I'm not sure which I would choose as the brighter."

Act two: A social scientist has the student watch either a neutral film, nonviolent porn or some slimy concoction that shows a woman being raped violently (and apparently enjoying it).

Act three: The student sits at a machine and is ordered to question the same woman who pissed him off in act one. When she answers a question incorrectly, the student must give her an electric shock. By fiddling with a dial, the student can change the level of the shock.

Authority, Not Sex

In the original experiment, men who saw violent porn administered a higher level of shock to the woman than men who watched nonviolent erotica. To us the experiment proved one thing: If a person in a white lab coat tells you to do something, adding that it will help you learn, you'll do it. The experiment seems more about authority than about sex.

Obedience to authority, no matter what personal morality dictates, is a phenomenon psychologist Stanley Milgram documented in the Sixties. His experiments showed that people who were not normally cruel were quite capable of inflicting pain if told to do so by someone in authority. In following Milgram's research, other researchers found that people of both sexes were failing to administer shocks when they had nothing to gain or lose by refusing, even when the decision was left up to them. So if there is blame to lay, it is with the individual, not with the stimuli.

A Vital Difference

But that is not what the public wants to hear about pornography. And so, says Fisher, "the social scientists just said, 'In laboratory studies, exposure to pornography causes men to be physically aggressive against women.'"

No Link

Since the feminist censorship proposals aim at sexually explicit material that allegedly is "degrading" to women, it is especially noteworthy that research data show no link between exposure to "degrading" sexually explicit material and sexual aggression.

Nadine Strossen, *Defending Pornography: Free Speech, Sex, and the Fight for Women's Rights*, 1995.

Fisher re-created the experiment with one vital difference: "I sat the guys in front of the shock generator. At this point in the original experiment—and this is the killer issue—the guys had no choice. I asked myself, What if they could just walk away? What if they could talk to the woman?"

Fisher gave 14 men the choice to leave. Twelve did. Real men don't put up with bullshit experiments.

Were the two others rapists? No, says Fisher. "One of them was a computer hacker, sort of a computer hobbyist; the other was a ham radio operator. They were mechanically inclined. Both saw the shock generator before the experiment and said, 'Can't wait to use it.'"

No Real Correlation

Real men leave. Maybe because the woman pissed them off or tried to fry their balls or because in the face of insult, they calculated that there was little chance of getting laid. Maybe they just went somewhere to masturbate. As for the techno-dweebs? Boys love toys. On a talk show devoted to bias in social science research, Fisher described another approach to this experiment:

"Say we were to run experiments in which a woman received massive exposure to soap operas and was then told to press a button that would result in a man somewhere being nagged. If we wrote this up, saying that soap operas cause women to nag men, we would justifiably be laughed at. But because the artificial experimentation of the original study dovetailed with prevailing wisdom about 'Men: Threat or Menace,' it got wide play in the literature."

"I was not a willing participant [in pornography]. There were guns, there were knives, there were beatings, there were threats on the lives of my family."

Pornography Harms Those Involved in Its Production

Linda Marchiano

Linda Marchiano appeared as Linda Lovelace in the pornographic film *Deep Throat*. She is also the author of *Ordeal*, an account of her experiences in the pornography industry. In the following viewpoint, which is excerpted from testimony before the Attorney General's Commission on Pornography (the Meese Commission), Marchiano describes being coerced into participating in pornography by means of mental abuse, beatings, and threats against herself and her family. Marchiano insists that although she appears to be enjoying herself in *Deep Throat*, she was in fact brutalized and traumatized during the film's production.

As you read, consider the following questions:
1. What does Marchiano say happened the first three times she tried to escape from Charles Trainor?
2. How does Marchiano explain the fact that she appears to enjoy herself in the film?

Excerpted from Linda Marchiano's testimony before the Attorney General's Commission on Pornography, January 21, 1986, New York, New York.

It all began in 1971. I was recuperating from a near-fatal automobile accident at my parents' home in Florida. A girlfriend of mine came over to visit me with a person by the name of Mr. Charles Trainor. Mr. Trainor came off as a very considerate gentleman, asking us what we would like to do and how we would like to spend our time and our afternoons, opening doors and lighting cigarettes and doing all the so-called good manners of society. Needless to say, I was impressed and started to date him.

I was not at the time getting along with my parents. I was twenty-one years old and was resenting being told to be home at 11:00 and to call and say where I was and give them the number and address.

The Biggest Mistake

Here comes the biggest mistake of my life. Seeing how upset I was with my home life, Mr. Trainor offered his assistance. He said I could come and live at his house in north Miami. The relationship at this time was platonic, which was just fine with me. My plan was to recuperate and to go back to New York and live the life that I was living before my accident.

I thought then that he was being kind and a nice friend. Today I know why the relationship was platonic. He was incapable of any kind of sexual act without inflicting some kind of degradation or pain on another human being. When I decided to head back for home and informed Mr. Trainor of my intention, that was when I met the real Mr. Trainor and my two and a half years of imprisonment began. He beat me physically and mentally from that day forward. He made a complete turnaround. I literally became a complete prisoner of his. I was not allowed out of sight or allowed to use a bathroom without his permission. When speaking to either my friends or my parents, he was on the extension with his Walther PPK .45 automatic 8-shot pointed at me.

The Ordeal of Pornography

I was beaten physically and suffered mental abuse each and every day. In my book *Ordeal*, which is an autobiography, I go into greater detail of the atrocities that I was put through, from prostitution to porno films to celebrity satisfier. The things that he used to get me involved in pornography ranged from this PPK Walther .45 automatic 8-shot and an M-16 semiautomatic machine gun to threats on the lives of my friends and my family. I have seen the kind of people involved in pornography and how they will use anyone to get what they want.

The coldness and the callousness that they possess is immense. So many people asked me why I didn't escape. Well, I did, because I am here today. I did try, during my two and a half years, to escape, on three separate occasions. The first and second time I suffered a brutal beating for trying. The third time I was at my parents' house, and Mr. Trainor came over and he said that if I didn't go with him he would kill my parents and I said that, no, he wouldn't do that, and he said that I will shoot every member of your "blank" family as they come through the door. And then at that time my nephew came crawling into the room, and I got up and left with Mr. Trainor.

Some of you might say that I was foolish for going with Mr. Trainor, but I am not the kind of a person that could have lived the rest of my life knowing that it was possible because somebody else's life was taken.

After three unsuccessful attempts at escaping, I realized that I had to create a so-called master plan. It took six months of preparation convincing Mr. Trainor that I thought what he was saying was right, that beating people was the right thing to do, that abusing humans was proper, that pornography was great.

Lucky to Stay Sane

From the age of four to sixteen, I was used in pornographic magazines and films. My father, his friends, my uncles, and my grandfather made pornography using my mother, myself and numerous other women and children. . . . My father and his allies spent years training me. They trained me like you train a dog, a puppy, only I was much less than a dog. . . . Next to nothing. . . . Nothing at all. The bright lights and the pictures for sale of my pain, my pain shattered like glass. A thousand pieces, a thousand printings of the rapes. Immortalized. Eternal. Sold, laughed at, . . . fantasized over, and the profit went to my father, my uncles, my grandfather and I was lucky if I got food and I was lucky to stay alive and I was lucky to stay sane.

Anonymous, *Off Our Backs*, April 1993.

Fortunately for me, after six months I acquired fifteen minutes out of his presence, but I also had someone who wanted to help me.

I tried to tell my story several times, once to Vern Scott, who is a UPI reporter, and he told me that he couldn't print it. I also tried to tell a program in California what had happened to me, and they just changed the subject.

After my final escape, I was hiding out and I also tried to call the Beverly Hills Police Department, and I asked them to do something. I tried to tell them my story, and they told me to call back when he was in the room with his .45 or his M-16. I was brought up on obscenity charges in California.

A grand jury watched the film [*Deep Throat*] while I tried to black out what I was seeing and remembering and feeling the day that film was being shot.

After they asked me why I did it, I told them that a gun was influencing me, and they said, "Oh." No charges were filed against Mr. Trainor, and I was acquitted because it was done against my will.

Somehow pornography has brought me here today. All I can do is tell you my story and what happened to me. I was a victim of pornography.

Not a Willing Participant

Dr. Park Dietz: You mentioned several details about the firearms involved. Why did you mention the details about them?

Marchiano: Well, because I think it's very important for people to know that I was not a willing participant. There were guns, there were knives, there were beatings, there were threats on the lives of my family constantly, and after the physical abuse, the mental abuse becomes just as damaging. I just think it's important that people realize that. So many people that produce these types of films will say, Well, we check out and make sure that these women are doing it willingly.

But you know, I always ask them, had Mr. Trainor come with Linda Lovelace ten years ago, would you have known that she was an unwilling participant? So how can they say that they make sure all the women are there willingly?

Dietz: It's been said that the behavior that you evidenced in the film *Deep Throat* looks to others as being inconsistent with one being coerced. I wonder if you would care to comment on how that came about.

Marchiano: Well, I learned very quickly with Mr. Trainor to do exactly what I was told to do and do it to the best of my ability and to be convincing, because if I did become emotional, I ended up crying, or, you know, not looking like I was really enjoying myself, and then I suffered a brutal beating, some kind of sexual perversion as punishment, and I would have to do it anyway. So my mother didn't raise me as a total fool. I realized what I would have to do is be convincing and do it and get it over with. That whole film was done in that way. Everything was done just one time.

Dietz: Did you undergo any beatings during the course of the filming?

Marchiano: Yes, as a matter of fact, after the first day of shooting I suffered a brutal beating in my room, and the whole crew of the film was in the next room.

There was a door joining the rooms, and we were in this

room, they were in this room, and Mr. Trainor started pushing me around and punching me. I was smiling on the set too much that day, and then he started bouncing me off the walls and kicking me.

Well, I figured, if all these people were in the other room, maybe now somebody will help me. I will scream for help. And the only thing that happened was the room became very silent, and that was it.

The next day, they listened to him continue to beat me—and the next day the greatest complaint was I had a couple of bruises on my leg. You brought up the smile in *Deep Throat*, but nobody ever asked me how did I get those bruises, where did those bruises come from, how did they get there. Everybody always says, "Well, you got there, you smiled, you looked like you were having a good time." That smile is what saved my life.

Dietz: What was done to cover up the bruises?

Marchiano: One of the guys that was on the film, Mr. Reams, was also into stage makeup and all that, and he had the right kind of pancake or whatever they do. They just put layers and layers on it to try to cover it, but it still shows through.

> *"An intelligent, sexual woman could choose a job in the sex industry and not be a victim, but instead emerge even stronger and more self-confident."*

Pornography Does Not Always Harm Those Involved in Its Production

Leora Tanenbaum

Many opponents of pornography maintain that women who appear in pornographic films are unwilling participants who are abused and tortured. This is not always true, Leora Tanenbaum argues in the following viewpoint. Tanenbaum writes that many women choose to work in the pornography industry. These women enjoy their work and do not consider themselves victims, she asserts. Tanenbaum is a regular contributor to *In These Times*, a weekly newspaper of liberal political and social opinion.

As you read, consider the following questions:

1. Why does Tanenbaum reject the idea that Linda Marchiano was a victim of pornography?
2. What experiences of Candida Royalle show that the women in pornography are not coerced, according to Tanenbaum?
3. On what should antipornography feminists focus their efforts, in the author's opinion?

Leora Tanenbaum, "Forced Arguments," *In These Times*, March 7, 1994. Reprinted with permission.

If pornography is demeaning to women, then why do so many of them choose to enter the porn industry? To anti-porn feminists, the answer is simple: they don't. Since no one could possibly want to work in porn, the choice is made for them: they are coerced.

And, once there, these women are abused—or so anti-porn feminists allege. As Catharine MacKinnon has written memorably in her book *Only Words:* "In mainstream media, violence is done through special effects; in pornography, women shown being beaten and tortured report being beaten and tortured." But she goes beyond the simple cataloging of indictable offenses; for her, pornography itself is figured as a kind of abuse. Gloria Steinem has similarly argued: "Pornography is not about sex. It's about an imbalance of male-female power that allows and even requires sex to be used as a form of aggression."

A more familiar accusation is that porn is dangerous because the men who consume it are incited to assault women. Numerous researchers have purported to demonstrate this link, but the studies reveal contradictory findings. "The fast-accumulating research on the effects of violent pornography is most notable only for its inconsistency," Lynne Segal writes in *Sex Exposed.* "Although many sex offenders do use pornography, in general . . . they have had access to it at a later age than non sex-offenders, and are overwhelmingly more likely to have been punished for looking at it as teenagers."

The charge of coercion, by contrast, has wide resonance because it confirms pervasive stereotypes. And, of course, there are no social science studies that can refute the accusations of abuse in the production of porn: we who are outside the sex industry can rely only upon the reports of insiders.

Porn as Power

Yet these narratives do not always describe lives of exploitation and degradation. Some porn performers, in fact, claim to find their work enjoyable and empowering, positioning themselves as political resistance fighters. Nina Hartley, for example, started stripping in San Francisco in 1983. Now, at 32, she is a porn star, with hundreds of films to her credit. She is proud of her job, and defends it in consciously feminist terms, explaining that the porn industry "provides a surprisingly flexible and supportive arena for me to grow in as a performer, both sexually and non-sexually." Hartley became convinced early on that "an intelligent, sexual woman could choose a job in the sex industry and not be a victim, but instead emerge even stronger and more self-confident, with a feeling, even, of self-actualization." And for her, this has been true.

Not all in the industry are quite so sanguine. I.S. Levine, writer and director of more than 150 pornographic movies, chides Hartley for presenting a too-rosy picture of an industry he knows well. "Nina gets up there with a baseball bat ready to take on anyone with anything bad to say about the X-rated business, but it gets in the way of the truth, which is both more interesting and more useful," he told researcher Robert Stoller. "The public's idea about this industry is probably not far removed from the kind of industry it is: exploitative, with marginal personalities who can't integrate into society, self-destructive people living self-destructive lives."

Just a Job

Ginger put herself through New York University performing in peepshows and maintains that the shows are innocuous fun. "It's a safe, harmless way to have some erotica in one's life. It is certainly victimless and should be accepted in society.". . . Many people in the porn business say the performers are just people working a job. Alan, who owns a peep emporium, . . . says the women come from many walks of life. "There are a lot of college girls, women that have straight professions."

Wes Goodman, *USA Today*, March 1994.

It is no accident, certainly, that the women who choose jobs in the sex industry *are* often victims of some kind—of incest, drug addiction, poverty, low self-esteem, feelings of powerlessness. But does pornography *cause* their victimization? According to anti-porn feminists, these women would otherwise pursue mainstream jobs if they were not sucked into a misogynistic industry and kept there through abuse.

The most celebrated account of sexual coercion during the filming of an X-rated movie has been provided by Linda Lovelace (now Marchiano), the star of 1972's *Deep Throat*. Her 1980 autobiography, *Ordeal*, tells a harrowing story of daily torture. Marchiano was routinely raped, beaten, kicked and choked. She was forced to have sex with a dog for a low-budget porn movie; when she protested, she was told, "You make this movie or you're going to die."

But it was Marchiano's *husband*, Chuck Traynor, who abused her—not the pornographers. Traynor forced her to have sex with clients he solicited, beating her and pointing a gun at her head when she struggled. In order to increase her value as a prostitute, Traynor hypnotized her and taught her "deep throating," an oral sex technique based on his knowledge of sword-swallowing. She wasn't allowed to call or visit her parents; she wasn't even allowed to go to the bathroom or to sleep without Traynor's permission.

In fact, Marchiano's career as a porn star helped her to escape, at least temporarily, from the brutality of her husband. In *Ordeal*, she describes the sense of freedom she felt on the set of *Deep Throat*. She enjoyed the company of her co-star, Harry Reems. "Something was happening to me, something strange," she wrote. "No one was treating me like garbage. . . . We laughed a lot that first day of shooting. . . . And no one was asking me to do anything I didn't want to do." No one, that is, but her husband—who was so threatened by his wife's evident enjoyment that he brutally beat her after the first day of shooting, throwing her against their hotel room wall and kicking her for hours until he was too tired to continue.

Faulty Feminist Logic

Feminists against pornography have deliberately misinterpreted *Ordeal*, twisting its facts to suit their agenda. They hold up Marchiano's story as proof *par excellence* of the abusive working conditions within the porn industry. MacKinnon uses Marchiano's life story to serve her own faulty logic: "If a woman had to be coerced to make *Deep Throat*, doesn't that suggest that *Deep Throat* is dangerous to all women anywhere near a man who wants to do what he saw in it?" (Well, no.) And Andrea Dworkin asks in *Ms.* magazine's roundtable discussion on pornography: "Why did a woman have to be brutalized to make that film?" The answer is: she didn't. *Ordeal* makes this clear.

In the years following the publication of *Ordeal*, though, Marchiano has been all too willing to accommodate her anti-porn sisters. When she appeared on *Geraldo* in 1988, Marchiano spoke of her experience working on *Deep Throat* in the passive voice, obfuscating the source of her coercion: "I was beaten and I was forced into it, and I had a .45 pointed at me, an M-16 semiautomatic machine gun," she told the audience. "I was beaten on a daily basis, the threats—constant threats on the lives of my parents and my family and friends, and my life. . . . I was raped in that movie." Not once did she mention that the abuser was her husband.

Candida Royalle, who starred in over a dozen X-rated movies in the '70s before she became a director of alternative porn in the '80s, knows that there are loathsome people in the industry, and that it can feel dirty and shameful to work for them. She also admits that many of the women who do porn work lack self-esteem and economic resources.

But coercion? That's a different story. The only places Royalle ever faced sexual harassment were in "straight" jobs. When she was 17, working as a receptionist at a health club in New York, she was sexually assaulted by her boss. At 19, when she worked at Ticketron, her employer made her kiss him good night every night in order to keep her job.

"I was never forced to do anything in pornography," she told me. "The closest I ever came to any attempt at coercion was during a film I made with a very famous director, about a guy who had abused prostitutes, who were now getting back at him. The women were all supposed to stand on him and urinate on him. So the director was passing out beers. I was like, What is this? 'This is the, uh, urination scene.' I was like, Excuse me? I not only refused to do it, I organized all the other women and said, 'We're not going to do anything we don't want to do.' Four of the women did agree because they had no problem with it, but the rest of us didn't. The director was very angry, and said I would never work for him again, and that was fine."

Royalle is critical of those feminists who want to "protect" women like her. "I understand their desire to help women, but they are out of touch with women in the industry," she told me. "You go out and talk to most of the women in California, and they would say, 'How dare you tell me I can't do this. How dare you threaten to take away an income for work that I enjoy doing.'"

Women are indeed exploited in the porn industry, she notes, "because we are absolutely necessary for the production, yet our sexuality is completely ignored." Royalle does not consider pornography dangerous or horrible—but she is insulted by most of what she sees.

Porn for Women

So she has taken control of the way women's sexuality is represented in porn. Her downtown Manhattan production company, Femme, creates and distributes sexually explicit films geared to women and heterosexual couples. Royalle's work is different from the mainstream. Her movies never jump right into the sex; Royalle prefers instead to create suspense. "I want to tell men and women: wait a minute, slow down, there is so much beautiful stuff you're racing past." She portrays strong, assertive female characters—and men who aren't intimidated by them. In an effort to depict egalitarian sex, she is careful never to show force or violence, and the one bondage scene she has shot, in *Three Daughters* (1986), is so sensitively consensual as to be, she laughs, "milk toast."

But when Royalle debated two women from the Canadian censor board, one of them accused her of promoting violence against women with the *Three Daughters* scene. The government subsequently made her eliminate that sequence from the Canadian version of the movie. "And I find that very damaging to people's sexuality," Royalle laments. "It drives home a terrible message: that I am sick for having that fantasy."

It is clear, then, that the charge of violence and coercion is just a cover: the central concern of the anti-porn feminists is sex, not sexism, and the real target is sexual representation *of any kind*. No wonder they focus on sexually explicit materials, even though other media are equally, if not more, sexist.

As long as there are poor women, there will be sex work, and this work will be degrading mainly to the extent that the women entering the profession are desperate. Even Nina Hartley admits, in a self-reflective moment, that "the concept of 'choice' depends a lot on one's class background and many sex workers (as with workers in all fields) might desire to make their living in other ways if there were real options available." Would feminists against pornography contentedly pack up their petitions and megaphones, I wonder, if porn actresses left the business to work as domestic servants and burger-flippers? Anti-pornography organizers would do better to focus their efforts on changing the conditions that force economically deprived people to take degrading jobs in the first place.

Periodical Bibliography

The following articles have been selected to supplement the diverse views presented in this chapter. Addresses are provided for periodicals not indexed in the *Readers' Guide to Periodical Literature*, the *Alternative Press Index*, or the *Social Sciences Index*.

Robert L. Allen	"Out of the Bedroom Closet," *Ms.*, January/February 1992.
Walter Berns	"Learning to Live with Sex and Violence," *National Review*, November 1, 1993.
David Futrelle	"The Politics of Porn: Shameful Pleasures," *In These Times*, March 7, 1994.
Wes Goodman	"Pornography, Peep Shows, and the Decline of Morality," *USA Today*, March 1994.
Sharon Hancock	"Women Fight Back Against Abuse," *Citizen*, September 20, 1993. Available from Focus on the Family, PO Box 35500, Colorado Springs, CO 80935-0550.
Tom Hess	"The Violent World of Pornography," *Citizen*, July 19, 1993.
Thomas Jipping	"Opening the Door to Child Pornography," *Family Voice*, December 1993. Available from Concerned Women for America, 370 L'Enfant Promenade SW, Suite 800, Washington, DC 20024.
John Paul II	"Pornography and the Exploitation of Individuals," *Origins*, February 13, 1992. Available from Catholic News Service, 3211 Fourth St. NE, Washington, DC 20017.
Berl Kutchinsky	"Pornography and Rape: Theory and Practice," *International Journal of Law and Psychiatry*, vol. 14, 1991.
Catharine A. MacKinnon	"Turning Rape into Pornography: Postmodern Genocide," *Ms.*, July/August 1993.
Wayne Maser	"Women Who Love Pornography," *Harper's Bazaar*, August 1994.
Moody	"Be Careful, Little Eyes," March 1995.

Should Pornography
Be Censored?

Pornography

Chapter Preface

Freedom of speech is guaranteed by the First Amendment to the U.S. Constitution. The government, however, has the power to restrict speech if its expression threatens to be destructive. It is often a challenge for the courts to determine whether a certain form of speech is potentially harmful and should therefore be curbed. This struggle has been especially difficult in the case of pornography.

Local, state, and federal obscenity laws regulate the production and distribution of some forms of pornography. Child pornography, for example, is assumed to be destructive and is therefore banned. Other forms of pornography, however, do not indisputably fall within definitions of obscenity. For example, the photographs of Robert Mapplethorpe, including male nudes in homosexual poses, are viewed as art by some people but are considered obscenity by others.

Some people argue that because the definition of obscenity is often subjective, pornography involving adults should not be subject to obscenity laws. Critics contend that this form of censorship allows a small number of government representatives to define obscenity for everyone else, which could lead to a gradual erosion of First Amendment rights. Ursula K. Le Guin, a noted author and poet, believes that pornography harms society and women. Nevertheless, she argues that society should oppose "*any* censorship—by decree or by lawsuit, by commercial, religious, or government interests, in the schools or in the marketplace. That means not silencing the pornographers and their advocates."

Others believe that pornography should be censored. They believe that pornography is a form of destructive speech and that censorship is justified as a means of protecting society from its harmful effects. Furthermore, advocates of obscenity laws contend that censorship of pornography does not threaten the public's First Amendment rights. As Mark Y. Herring, dean of library sciences at Oklahoma Baptist University, writes,

> How is it that if you censor, say, cybersex fellatio, our Constitution ends in shambles?. . . Our Founding Fathers never intended that the First Amendment be taken to mean that any and all modes of communication should be unrestrained and readily accessible. We seem either unable, unwilling, or a little of both, to make any intellectual distinction between liberty on the one hand, and libertinage on the other.

The following chapter explores the question of whether pornography should be censored, and if so, to what extent. The authors present their views on how society should balance the right to free speech with the need to protect the public from possibly harmful words and images.

"*Failure to act sends the message . . . that the pornography and sleaze do not violate community standards.*"

Pornography Should Be Censored

Robert W. Peters

In the following viewpoint, Robert W. Peters argues that pornography is harmful and that all Americans should be active in opposing its production and distribution. According to Peters, government, businesses, churches, and citizens all have a responsibility to censor pornography through legislation and through political and personal actions. Peters is the president of Morality in Media, Inc., a national interfaith organization that works to curb traffic in illegal hard-core pornography.

As you read, consider the following questions:

1. What can businesses do to combat pornography, in the author's opinion?
2. According to Peters, what do most Americans think about pornography's effects on society?
3. Why is the government limited in its ability to fight pornography, according to the author?

Robert W. Peters, "Socially Speaking (Whose Responsibility Is It, Anyway?)" *Religious Broadcasting*, September 1995. Reprinted by permission from National Religious Broadcasters.

Whether the subject is pornography in "cyberspace" or sex, violence and vulgarity on TV or in films, rock music and RAP, the question keeps coming up, "Whose responsibility is it anyway?"

Not surprisingly, the "candidates" for shouldering the responsibility vary depending on the ideological and religious views of those who make the selection.

Many in the media and entertainment industries acknowledge that they have a responsibility. Most, however, still say that they are just providing what the public wants and that if the public stops buying, they will stop providing. Both industries also oppose any government intervention.

Political liberals usually oppose government involvement, although some make exceptions for TV violence and pornography that is degrading to women. Many political liberals are also reluctant to blame the media and entertainment industries, fearing an angry backlash will lead to "censorship."

For many political conservatives, the guiding principle appears to be "the less government, the better"—even in areas where government has traditionally exercised its police power to protect what the Supreme Court has called "the social interest in order and morality" and the right to "maintain a decent society."

Religious conservatives are far more likely to place most of the blame on the industries which produce and distribute offensive entertainment and to support government intervention. Many, however, don't seem to understand that much depends on them.

Everyone Is Responsible

In my view, businesses, citizens and parents, government and the churches are ALL responsible.

Just as individual citizens have legal rights and responsibilities, so do businesses. For example, Federal and state laws prohibit obscenity. Indecency is also prohibited or regulated in bars, on TV, dial-a-porn services and in other circumstances.

To be a good citizen and neighbor, however, more is required than avoiding criminal prosecution. Businesses, like the people that run them, have moral as well as legal responsibilities.

Much pornography is protected by the First Amendment, as are many other forms of exploitive "entertainment" that can be injurious to others. Film and TV producers, record companies and publishers, as well as the businesses that distribute their products, have a right to refuse to provide such "entertainment." This is good citizenship, not "censorship."

Opinion polls continue to show that most citizens and, in particular, parents view pornography as harmful and gratuitous sex, violence and vulgarity in the media as having a negative effect, particularly where children are concerned.

But awareness must be "translated" into constructive action. Responsible citizens shouldn't be viewing pornography and sleaze, and responsible parents should be doing all they can to shield their children from entertainment harmful to them.

Reprinted by permission: Tribune Media Services.

Complaints should be made to the producers and distributors, and, whenever possible, responsible citizens and parents should avoid doing business with companies that ignore those complaints.

When appropriate, responsible citizens and parents should also be insisting that law enforcement agencies investigate for possible violations of Constitutional laws against obscenity or indecency.

Anti-pornography Laws Are Needed

Government too has a vital role to play, because no matter how much most businesses try to be responsible citizens and how much most citizens and parents try to avoid pornography and trashy "entertainment," some will fail and others will not try at all.

The reason we have laws is, in the words of the Apostle Paul,

68

not "for a righteous man" but "for the lawless and disobedient." And, contrary to the propaganda spread by the American Civil Liberties Union (ACLU) and mainstream media, not every law that punishes speech is unconstitutional or a threat to our cherished First Amendment freedoms.

As pointed out by the Supreme Court in a 1954 obscenity case, "the unconditional phrasing of the First Amendment was not intended to protect every utterance." And, it never will.

Clearly, however, where speech and press are concerned, the government's powers are limited—which is why businesses, citizens, parents and churches must also share the responsibility.

How can it be that those who go to church purchase and even sell pornography, and nothing is ever said from the pulpit? How can it be that those who are commanded to love their neighbors stand idly by while their communities are flooded with pornography and with mindless sex and violence, packaged as "entertainment?"

It is up to the churches to fight the purveyors of pornography and sleaze, and one way to do so is by participating in the annual White Ribbon Against Pornography (WRAP) Campaign, which Morality in Media and other groups promote during Pornography Awareness Week, Oct. 29 to Nov. 5.

Failure to act sends the message either that the pornography and sleaze do not violate community standards or that we lack the will or courage to combat what the writer of Proverbs called "a reproach to any people" (Proverbs 14:34).

"Groups seeking to censor explicit sexuality should redirect their energy at censoring violence."

Only Violent Pornography Should Be Censored

Pete Marksteiner

Many people believe that all pornography should be censored. In the following viewpoint, Pete Marksteiner contends that pornography comes in two distinct forms: depictions of sex and depictions of violence. Marksteiner argues that violence, not sex, is the real danger to society. He cites studies that suggest that viewing violence causes people to think and act violently, while viewing sex has no negative effect. Based on these findings, he concludes that violent pornography should be legally censored but that nonviolent pornography should be subjected to no such regulation. Marksteiner is an attorney in Cheyenne, Wyoming.

As you read, consider the following questions:

1. Why does Marksteiner believe the anti-pornography movement lacks credibility?
2. What does the author mean when he says that anti-pornography absolutists base their arguments on "self-declared enlightenment"?
3. What were the specific results of the study Marksteiner describes concerning the effects of viewing violence and sex?

From Pete Marksteiner, "The Ongoing Pornography Debate," *Washburn Law Journal*, vol. 34, no. 1, Fall 1994. Reprinted with permission.

"My God," Fanny would say later, "They bring their daughter to see a murder, but they wouldn't even let her hear about an orgasm. Americans sure are strange."

John Irving, *The Hotel New Hampshire*, 1981

Whether, or to what extent, pornography harms women is a topic of ongoing debate in this country and in others. The most cursory glance at the available literature on the topic reveals that opinions on the subject vary dramatically. Some commentators assert a direct causal link between pornography and violence against women. Some include pornography as one of several factors which should be considered in a causal model, while others [such as author Martin D. Schwartz] argue that "pornography is only a symptom [of something else], not a problem and unworthy of such extensive feminist attention. . . ."

The debate has fostered the creation of some unlikely alliances as well as some curious divisions among ideological camps. For example, it seems at least a little odd to find glowing praise of Catharine MacKinnon in what most would call radically *conservative* anti-pornography literature. On the other hand, the pornography debate frequently pits feminist against feminist. . . .

The Two Arguments

The pro-porn advocates usually couch their arguments in first amendment or privacy rhetoric. They also rely heavily on empirical studies, the overwhelming majority of which solidly dispute any connection between non-violent erotica and harm to women.

The anti-porn absolutists make an epistemological argument which is all but impossible to respond to. The argument may be stated as follows: Our social institutions legitimize patriarchy, and people who are surrounded by these institutions from cradle to grave internalize a model of patriarchy and male dominance as the baseline norm. Empirical studies simply validate that skewed norm, and those who do not recognize the correctness of the anti-porn absolutists have yet to cast away their patriarchally tainted perception of reality. This theme, though seldom explicitly stated, runs throughout anti-porn absolutist literature. . . .

Both arguments are persuasive, and both arguments support the conclusion reached in this viewpoint, that violent pornography should be legally censored. It should be noted here that the question of what is violent is admittedly broad, and that according to some authors, heterosexual sex is by its very nature violent. "Violent," for the purposes of this viewpoint, should be understood to describe depictions wherein participants are presented as being forced, against their will, to participate, or where participants are physically injured.

The anti-porn absolutists lose a great deal of credibility when they completely refuse to recognize any differences between the respective harms caused by the separate spheres of erotica and violent pornography. It is one thing to say that both types of materials have harmful effects; it is quite another to claim that there is no difference between the two. As Allison Assister writes, "[One] should surely not be expected to take women's outrage at the center spread in *Playboy* magazine as on a par with the emotions of the woman who has undergone the horrific experience of a rape." Surely there is a recognizable difference.

Sex and Violence—Are They the Same?

The anti-porn absolutists also seem to exaggerate the amount of pornography that contains violence. While a great deal of pornography is indisputably based on sexist objectification, violence and objectification are not the same thing.

> The women [in four popular soft core magazines] are not being physically hurt by anyone nor, indeed are they being psychologically or emotionally intimidated. On the contrary, the women are represented as enjoying themselves, and not in a masochistic manner. . . . This is the degradation of women, the downplaying of women's intelligence and abilities, the denial that they are real human beings, but it is not subjecting women to violence. [Allison Assister]

Andrea Dworkin asserts that sexuality and violence are the fundamentals of male power. "[A] saber penetrating a vagina is a weapon . . . so is the penis for which it substitutes (vagina literally means 'sheath')." Debra L. Olsson states, "The purposes of man stand[] in total opposition to those of women." Other commentators take a similar, though somewhat more watered down, approach: "[T]here has been a general tendency within feminism to view all forms of perversion as symptoms of male sexuality and all forms of heterosexuality as tainted by perversion," Linda Williams writes. In fact, Jane Gallop states, many feminists end up . . . say[ing] that normal feminist sexuality is that of the lesbian—an egalitarian and tender sexuality of the 'whole person'—and that heterosexuality, the ostensible norm, is actually perverse." If the anti-porn absolutists recognize a reality which dictates that any sexual relation between a man and a woman entails some form of injurious degradation, then the absolutist argument becomes more persuasive. Once heterosexual sex is defined as violence, the exaggerated generalizations about the amount of violence in porn become more credible. . . .

The substantive meat of the anti-porn absolutist argument seems twofold. First, a person cannot consent—in the real sense of the word—to an activity which is injurious to that person. That premise, applied to pornography, essentially proceeds: (1) Prostitution is indisputably harmful; (2) A person cannot truly consent to participate in an activity that is harmful to that person; (3) People cannot truly consent to take part in prostitution; (4) Pornography is prostitution where a camera happens to be present; (5) People cannot truly consent to take part in pornography. Second, pornography bolsters the status quo which objectifies and devalues women, resulting in very real harm to women as a class.

Violence Incites Rape

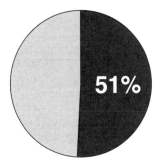

In a study by Seymour Feshback at UCLA, male students were exposed to violent pornography. After the exposure, 51% indicated the likelihood of raping a woman if assured they would not get caught.

Source: National Coalition for the Protection of Children and Families, 1995.

The first claim, that people could not possibly consent to something which is indisputably harmful, could be made about a number of activities other than participating in the creation of pornography. The persuasive weight of the claim depends to a great extent on the situationally specific characterization chosen to describe the behavior. For example, to frame the characterization, as Martin D. Schwartz does, "Some women must have sex with dirty, strange men so that they can have enough money to live . . ." conjures up a tragic image of a person's victimization. On the other hand, "whether or not a movie personality will allow *Playboy* to come into her multi-million dollar home to photograph her partially clothed for many thousands of dollars" conjures up a situation in one's mind which looks much different.

People routinely choose to engage in activities which are potentially harmful to themselves. Consider an average smoker, for example. A smoker voluntarily engages in a practice that chisels away minutes, days, months, and even years of his or her life with each successive puff. Tens of thousands of people each year sentence themselves to slow, agonizingly painful deaths resulting from a behavior they voluntarily, consensually engage in. How could anyone possibly consent to prematurely end his or her life in this manner? The same could be said about alcohol, a host of other drugs, even—in the extreme—a person's dietary practices. The Constitution safeguards an individual's right to make certain self determinative choices regardless of what his neighbor might think about the wisdom of his choice.

Defining Coercion

Florida has sought to create a legal framework which grants a civil cause of action to a person whose unwise choice was improperly influenced by a named bad actor. Specifically, the law gives a prostitute a cause of action against the person who coerced him or her into prostitution. The statute lists several definitions of coercion which common sense would dictate, such as actual or threatened force, kidnapping, etcetera. Additionally, there are a number of other activities which also qualify as actionable coercion under the statute, including promises of financial rewards and marriage, and exploitation of human needs for affection, that seem rather dubious. By defining things like witholding affection and promises of marriage as actionably coercive under the law, Florida has taken the first step backwards on the road to sexual equality. The law paints females (the preamble specifically recognizes that the majority of prostitutes are female) as emotional pillars of jello, requiring special protection from the world's evils, such as unsavory offers of marriage and money. When laws begin to construct protective fences around women in response to their *presumed* particular vulnerability to emotional and financial temptations, it is difficult to say that such a step is a positive one for women.

The pro-porn commentators, along with the ACLU [American Civil Liberties Union], the United States Supreme Court, the Florida Constitution, and many others have embraced an idea involving a person's right to be let alone. The right of self-determination, and its close cousin, the right of privacy, have been invoked to vindicate "personal choice" in a number of areas including, most notably for women, reproductive choice. The anti-porn absolutists find themselves joining forces in some rather unlikely alliances.

> [I]t certainly gives one pause to consider that Catharine Mac
> Kinnon [one of the leading anti-porn absolutist voices] assisted
> with the conservative and fundamentalist agenda of council-
> woman Beulah Coughenour, an anti-abortion activist and for-
> mer chairperson of the "Stop ERA" campaign, in an effort to
> enact the model anti-pornography legislation in Indianapolis.

Rhetorically, National Right to Life ("NRL") makes the same argument that the anti-porn absolutists make. According to

NRL, Pro-Choice folks have internalized the ethics of self-determinism—"autoarchy," although they do not realize that abortion is absolutely harmful to themselves (spiritually, and some would argue psychologically) and others (the unborn children they carry), we, who have been able to cast away the status quo—institutional autoarchy—know the truth. The truth is that abortion is harmful, to women and society, and it is incumbent upon us to take action to stop *all* abortions. This same rationale, that women are simply incapable of making certain decisions, has been used to oppress women throughout history. Justice Bradley, in his concurring opinion in *Bradwell v. Illinois* (1873), wherein the United States Supreme Court upheld Illinois' denial of bar admission to a woman, stated, "[T]he natural and proper timidity and delicacy which belongs to the female sex evidently unfits it for many of the occupations of civil life." The first claim in the anti-porn absolutist substantive argument, that women simply cannot consent to certain activities, does not fare well under close scrutiny.

Difficult to Prove Harm

The second claim, that all pornography harms women as a class, is difficult to support substantively. As discussed earlier, the empirical data not only absolutely fails to support the assertion that pornography harms women, the data provides affirmative evidence to the contrary. Because the data fails to support the anti-porn absolutists' position, commentators like Susan Brownmiller rhetorically ask questions like "do we really need studies to tell us what is obvious?" Questions like this lose their bite when one attempts to verify the obviousness of the harm she references.

It has already been established that the various methods of "proving" a claim about the wide-spread societal impacts of pornography are imperfect. It is by no means suggested here that empirical studies, alone, answer the question of whether pornography harms women. Nonetheless, if the negative effects of pornography are indeed as *obvious* as the anti-porn absolutists argue, one would certainly expect to find *some* identifiable manifestation in empirical data which is at least marginally accepted in the scientific community. The evidence is not there.

While a significant percentage of the scientific community does recognize a correlation between violent pornography and harm to women, the same cannot be said for non-violent erotica. Furthermore, one of the most recent studies sought to demonstrate the obvious effects non-violent erotica has on the status of women and found contrary results.

One side of the debate offers mountains of empirical evidence, time honored notions of freedom and privacy, and a common sense interpretation of the facts to support the assertion that non-violent erotica is not harmful to women. The other side, anti-porn absolutists, marshals a handful of empirical evidence, which has been widely criticized by the rest of the social science world, and its own common sense interpretation of the facts. The anti-porn absolutists then offer this questionable evidence to support the total prohibition of all material that falls within the extremely expansive range of "sexually harmful," with the precise guidelines defining that range knowable only by a tiny group of people who claim a sort of social omnipotence.

When the interests at stake are of the magnitude of those embodied in the rights of free expression, self-determination, and privacy, self-declared enlightenment is not a sufficient justification for jeopardizing those interests.

Focus Must Be on Violence

If the government is planning on legislating morality by increasing the regulations which govern what the public consumes through the print and film media, violence, not sexuality, should be the focus in the debate on pornography. All of the commentators, empiricists and non-empiricists alike, agree that certain depictions in print and film have a demonstrably causal relationship with violence—violence most commonly directed at women. Those depictions should be the subject of censorship efforts.

The social science literature is brimming with recommendations that groups seeking to censor explicit sexuality should redirect their energy at censoring violence. In one study, which approximates the collective body of work of many commentators, test subjects were shown erotica, violent pornography, and non-sexual, violence-only films. While the violent pornography group exhibited more callous attitudes toward rape victims than were exhibited by the erotica group, the group that had viewed violence-only films registered the most callous attitudes toward rape victims, as well as the highest self-reported likelihood of using force in a sexual encounter if they thought they could get away with it. The implication is clear; violence, rather than sexuality, is the precipitant of a socially undesirable result.

"Censorship is not the answer."

Pornography Should Not Be Censored

Susan Isaacs

The U.S. Constitution's First Amendment protects the right to free speech. This includes the right to produce, read, and view pornography, Susan Isaacs declares in the following viewpoint. While Isaacs agrees that some pornography is unappealing, she maintains that "to have speech we love, we have to defend speech we hate," including pornography. Isaacs is a member of the National Coalition Against Censorship and the author of several novels.

As you read, consider the following questions:

1. How does Isaacs respond to the argument that pornography incites violence?
2. What does the author mean when she says that blaming pornography for his crimes was an "easy out" for serial killer Ted Bundy?
3. What does the author fear will happen if government censorship of pornography is allowed?

Susan Isaacs, "Why We Must Put Up with Pornography," *Redbook*, August 1993. Copyright © 1993 by Susan Isaacs. Reprinted by permission of William Morris Agency, Inc., on behalf of the author.

If you and I were sitting together, listening to a little Vivaldi, sipping herbal tea, chatting about men and women, arguing about politics and art, we might get around to what to do about the porn problem—at which point you'd slam down your cup and demand, How can you of all people defend smut-peddling slimeballs who portray women being beaten and raped?

Well . . .

You're the one (you'd be sure to remind me) who hates any kind of violence against women. You're the one who even gets upset when James Cagney, in *The Public Enemy*, the 1931 classic, smashes a grapefruit into Mae Clarke's face, for heaven's sake.

That's right, I'd say.

So? Don't you want to protect women? Why not ban books and films that degrade women?

Let's have another cup of tea and I'll tell you.

Who Decides

The problem is, who is going to decide what is degrading to women? If there were to be a blue-ribbon panel, who would select its members? Jerry Falwell of the religious right? Andrea Dworkin, who has written that all sexual intercourse is an expression of men's contempt for women? They certainly do not speak for me. Okay, what about a blue-ribbon panel of, say, Hillary Rodham Clinton, Sandra Day O'Connor, Jackie Joyner-Kersee, Katie Couric, Wendy Wasserstein, and Anne Tyler? A dream team, right?

Sure. But I'll be damned if I'd hand over my right to determine what I see and read to America's best and brightest any more than I would to my husband, my editor, my best friend, or my mother. And you, my teasipping companion, and you, out there in Salt Lake City, Sioux City, Jersey City: You also should decide for yourself.

But, you might say next, this sexually explicit garbage eggs people on to vicious criminal behavior.

The truth is, this remains unproven. While research has pointed to a correlation between both alcohol abuse and dysfunctional families and violent behavior, it has not established the same link between pornography and violence. When serial killer Ted Bundy was trying to get his death sentence commuted in 1989, he claimed that a lifetime of reading pornography made him the monster he was. And why shouldn't he? It was an easy out: It would clear him of responsibility for his evil deeds.

But, you say, proof or no proof, there is so much trash out there and I don't like it. Well, neither do I, but censorship is not the answer. The First Amendment gives you the right to picket a theater or start a letter-writing campaign against any work you consider loathsome. You do not have the right, however, to prevent others from seeing it.

Look, it's rarely easy being a defender of the First Amendment. More often than not, we wind up fighting for the right to burn the flag, burn a cross or say awful racist and sexist things. Or consider a movie like *Boxing Helena*. It's about a doctor so obsessed with keeping a young woman all to himself that he amputates her legs and arms and keeps what's left of her in a box. Maybe it's art, maybe it's a disgusting, misogynistic piece of claptrap.

Steve Kelley. Reprinted with permission.

But if we want our great and beloved Constitution to work, we cannot abandon its principles when they don't suit us. To have speech we love, we have to defend speech we hate. Besides, most controversial material is open to more than one interpretation. To some, Robert Mapplethorpe's black-and-white photographs of nude men are breathtaking art; others think them immoral filth. In my own novel *Almost Paradise*, the heroine, as a child, is sexually abused by her father. This criminal betrayal colors her life. It was a nightmare for my character, and painful, even sickening, for me to write. Had some zealot been able to ban all references to incest—regardless of context or purpose—my novel would never have gotten written.

Censorship and Dictatorship

We can't hand over to anyone the power to decide what's appropriate for all. Because a year or a decade from now, someone might want to ban all depictions of career women or day-care centers, using the argument that they undermine family unity. Think that sounds extreme? Don't—historically, censorship has often been the first step toward dictatorship.

That's why we have to stand up for the First Amendment and not be moved, no matter how tempting it is to succumb to a just-this-once mentality. All of us, women and men, have to salute our Founding Fathers and say: Thanks for the legacy of freedom you gave us. And don't worry. We have the strength, the will, and yes, the guts to defend it.

"Censors think in terms of . . . the easiest, fastest solution. And the easiest, fastest solution penalizes all of us."

Obscenity Laws Threaten Free Speech

Dorothy Allison

Dorothy Allison, a novelist, is the author of several books, including *Skin: Talking About Sex, Class and Literature*. In the following viewpoint, Allison maintains that obscenity laws in Canada have restricted free speech and have abridged the rights of women, gays, and lesbians. While the author finds some pornographic material disgusting, she believes censorship in the form of obscenity laws poses a much greater threat to society than does pornography.

As you read, consider the following questions:

1. What were some of the works censored in Canada, according to Allison?
2. Why does the size of the publisher affect which books are prevented from entering Canada, according to the author?
3. What does the author mean when she says she fears the "power of outrage and impatience"?

Dorothy Allison, "The Porn Problem," *Glamour*, January 1995. Reprinted by permission of the Frances Goldin Literary Agency, for the author.

Like most of the women I know, I'm frankly disgusted by the glut of books, advertisements, films and even children's video games that rely on the callous brutalization of the female body. But I'm also a writer who wants women to have the freedom to explore—to talk about, write about, depict—sexual subjects. So I keep asking myself how we can preserve that freedom, while at the same time change the way our society misuses women's bodies.

In Canada, some antiporn activists believe they have found the answer. Because of their efforts, the Canadian Supreme Court ruled in 1992 in *Crown v. Butler* that printed or visual material "degrading" or "harmful" to women could be considered obscene. Graphic depictions of the sexual humiliation or rape of women could no longer be imported, sold or distributed— though, theoretically, serious artistic explorations of sexuality would remain untouched.

What has been the result? Canada already had a history of stopping "objectionable" literature at the border, but the court's decision emboldened customs officials to step up their activities. Since 1992, customs has seized or delayed shipment of, among other works:

- *The Man Sitting in the Corridor*, a novella by Marguerite Duras (author of *The Lover*, which won the Prix Goncourt, France's most prestigious literary prize).
- *Best Plays of Albert Innaurato*, which includes the Obie Award–winning *Gemini* and *The Transformation of Benno Blimpie*.
- *A Place I've Never Been*, a short-story collection by acclaimed fiction writer David Leavitt.
- *City of Night*, the classic underground novel of gay life by John Rechy.
- Black scholar bell hooks's award-winning study *Black Looks: Race and Representation*.

The Power of Some Pornographers

Ironically, two books by feminist antiporn activist Andrea Dworkin were also seized, presumably due to the examples of pornography that were contained within them.

What is not being seized: *Penthouse, Playboy*, pulp novels about serial killers who brutalize women's bodies. Why? For one thing, they're profitable for the Canadian economy. For another, their publishers have clout. Though there are exceptions on the list above, the majority of the books being stopped at the border are from small feminist, gay and other alternative presses that don't have expensive lawyers on retainer. Two books by novelist John Preston that were published by Alyson Publications, a Boston-based gay and lesbian press, were confiscated during the same period that his two erotic collections published by Penguin USA passed the border untouched.

What the censorship issue really comes down to is this: Who will make decisions for women? Who will decide what is degrading and harmful to us? Can we trust state employees to choose what we will be allowed to see or read? During the summer, many of Canada's border censors are college interns: young people with one day of training and little notion of what constitutes "harmful" or "degrading" beyond their own prejudices. My own collection of short stories, *Trash*, was detained for ten weeks not because of the content—no one at customs had actually read it—but because of the title. The clerk had confused my book with another by the same name, a collection of gay male fantasies with suggestive cover art.

The Rights of Consenting Adults

With potentially offensive materials readily available on cable television, on-line computer services and other media, many Americans are demanding more and more protections for children and other viewers. The push to create safeguards is understandable, but it should not be allowed to diminish the fundamental right to free expression or the equally basic right of consenting adults to decide for themselves what to watch or read.

With rare exceptions, the First Amendment ought to guarantee the right of Americans to produce, disseminate or view any kind of sexual material they want. That means the Government should intervene in only a narrowly defined set of circumstances—preventing the use of children in pornography depictions, for example, or restricting the flow of sexually explicit materials to children. . . . Existing laws provide ample authority to crack down on obscene material that raises no constitutional issues.

New York Times, October 1, 1995.

The lesson of the Canadian experience is that we cannot expect government to change how society thinks about and treats women. That's the work of citizens, parents, teachers, journalists, activists. We sometimes forget how fragile are the gains of the past couple of decades, forget how many people would like to return to the times when women had little or no access to books or art that encouraged them to become independent, strong, wild. Encouraging women to be strong is not what government agencies are about. No, bureaucrats and censors think in terms of checklists and the easiest, fastest solution. And the easiest, fastest solution penalizes all of us.

It is already arduous enough for an artist to try to address complicated subjects such as the development of female sexuality after sexual abuse—the topic I have been writing about for a decade. It took me a long time to complete my novel, *Bastard Out of Carolina*, the account of a strong but abused and deeply wounded 13-year-old. To write the book I first needed to find in *myself* a resilient and nourishing sexuality, in spite of the damage done by one brutal man in my life and by the (not unusual) childhood teaching that sex was too dangerous to be enjoyed. I needed the compassion and insights of "dangerous" books other women had written before me, books such as Toni Morrison's *The Bluest Eye* and Alice Walker's *The Color Purple*. If those works had not been available to me because of some harried bureaucrat's quick decision, I don't know that I would ever have been able to finish my own novel. Worse, I might have continued to be paralyzed by feelings of sexual shame.

The Wrong Law

Some writers and artists have argued that the *Butler* decision could never happen here—that America's First Amendment tradition protects us from that. I wish I were certain this were so, but I know the power of outrage and impatience, of that anxious desire to do something, anything. Next time you are shocked by some misogynist prose or cover art and hear yourself thinking, *There ought to be a law*, think again. It might not turn out to be the law you really want.

"Concerned citizens who are insisting that the constitutional obscenity laws be enforced . . . are not engaging in censorship."

Obscenity Laws Do Not Threaten Free Speech

Betty Wein

Many people oppose the censorship of pornography on the grounds that it violates the constitutional right to free speech. In the following viewpoint, Betty Wein contends that hard-core pornography, which is characterized by violence and pathological behavior, is illegal under current obscenity laws and is therefore not protected by the First Amendment. She concludes that obscenity laws are constitutional and that such laws should be enforced in order to rid society of hard-core pornography. Wein is the editor of *Morality in Media*, an organization that works to stop the traffic in pornography.

As you read, consider the following questions:

1. According to the U.S. Supreme Court, as cited by Wein, what three criteria must material meet in order to be obscene?
2. What are some of the tragic consequences of viewing pornography, in the author's opinion?
3. What steps can average Americans take to combat pornography, according to Wein?

Betty Wein, "Join the Fight Against Pornography!" *Morality in Media Newsletter*, July/August 1994. Reprinted by permission of the author.

How radically times have changed! Just yesterday, it seems, a person had to go out of his way to find hard-core pornography. Today, an increasing number of Americans have to go out of their way to avoid it.

Concerned parents all over the country are sounding the alarm that they can no longer protect their children, in this high-tech era, from the pornography industry. They are painfully aware that pornography is not just invading communities and neighborhoods but also slithering into the living rooms of this nation as dial-a-porn, video porn, cableporn, satellite porn, radio porn, computer porn and rock music porn.

The porn industry will immediately label anyone who joins the battle against pornography with the title "censor." Next comes the label of "prude." And then all the weary old cliches, such as "pornography is a victimless crime," will be dredged up and tossed at you.

Do not be intimidated by these tactics. Educate yourself instead! There are some basic truths you need to master to know your rights and to be able to defend them.

Pornographic material that is "obscene" (sometimes called "hardcore") is illegal on the federal level and in over forty states. The U.S. Supreme Court has said that to be "obscene," a video, magazine, performance or other "work" must meet the following three criteria: 1) the average person, applying contemporary community standards, must find that the work, taken as a whole, appeals to the prurient interest; 2) the work must depict or describe sexual conduct in a patently offensive way; and 3) the work, taken as a whole, must lack serious literary, artistic, political and scientific value.

More and more, the pornography polluting our communities is hardcore and a far cry from the pin-up girls with which many associate it. Reflecting the pathological side of human nature, hardcore pornography features sadomasochism; incest; bestiality; group sex; bisexuality; excretory activities; necrophilia and other abberations. Pornography, to be sure, has become more sick and violent.

The Public's Silence

Right about now, you must be wondering why this depraved material is being circulated with impunity if it is illegal. The answer to that can be summarized in three words: the public's silence!

The obscenity law is unique in that it is based, in part, on contemporary community standards. If law enforcement officials do not receive complaints from the community, they are prone to translate that silence into acceptance of the hardcore pornography being sold in your neighborhood.

That is why it is essential for you, and for any church, synagogue or civic group to which you belong, to register complaints with your district attorney (called county prosecutors or state's attorneys in some states) and ask him or her to investigate any hardcore pornographic outlets for possible violation of the state obscenity law.

As for the erroneous charge of "censorship," syndicated columnist Thomas Sowell calls it the most misused word in the English language. Here is the legal meaning of censorship: "prior restraint of First Amendment rights by government." Censorship is unconstitutional and illegal. The enforcement of the obscenity laws, however, is not censorship since the government is not exercising any prior restraint. Obscenity laws are enforced after publication, not before. Furthermore, obscenity is not a First Amendment right, any more than libel, perjury, contempt of court, false advertising, copyright violations or inciting a riot. The First Amendment has never been absolute!

The Pope's View on Pornography

The proliferation of pornographic literature is only one indication of a broader crisis of moral values affecting contemporary society. Pornography is immoral and ultimately antisocial. . . . By reducing the body to an instrument for the gratification of the senses, pornography frustrates authentic moral growth and undermines the development of mature and healthy relationships. It leads inexorably to the exploitation of individuals, especially those who are most vulnerable, as is so tragically evident in the case of child pornography.

Pope John Paul II, address to the Religious Alliance Against Pornography, January 1992.

Concerned citizens who are insisting that the constitutional obscenity laws be enforced to rid their communities of illegal hardcore pornography are not engaging in censorship. They are exercising their precious First Amendment rights to free speech, their rights to ward off assaults on their families, and their responsibilities to protect public morality, public safety and public health.

Morality in Media's phones ring daily with stories of pornography's victims. We frequently hear from parents whose children have been traumatized or corrupted by exposure to material unfit even for adults. Tragically, some of those children have tried to act out on other children what they have heard on dial-a-porn or seen in pornographic magazines or videos.

It is not uncommon to receive a distressed phone call from a woman whose marriage has gone sour due to her husband's porn addiction. We also hear from the addicted men themselves —tortured souls seeking help after the destruction of their marriage and loss of their children.

We get letters from prisoners, pouring out their hearts about how pornography triggered their sexual crimes and actually served as a blueprint for brutality. We also get many calls from people coast to coast who seek advice on how to cope with the emerging, so-called "adult" video stores and bookstores, destroying the quality of life in their communities, spitting in the face of family values and attempting to make a mockery of the Judeo-Christian code which has served as a cornerstone of Western civilization. No, pornography is not a victimless crime.

A Monster in Our Midst

There are also many laboratory-type studies that provide evidence of pornography's pernicious effects. One of the most common findings involves desensitization. The porn consumer soon becomes desensitized to violence, rape and the worst sexual aberrations.

"Too many decent grassroots Americans have been drifting and dreaming while a monster has grown in our midst," warned Morality in Media's late president, Father Paul Murphy, S.J. That monster, he said, is "the pornography industry."

What can you do in this war on families and your most cherished values? Undoubtedly, there is no need to tell you to monitor your children's TV viewing habits and also the music they listen to and the magazines they read—that is common sense in these decadent days.

However, you must also vocalize your concerns and outrage to those responsible for the pornographic assaults on your community and family. Otherwise, your silence will be interpreted as acceptance by law enforcement officials and merchants. Even worse, it may also be viewed as acceptance by your own children. And, your silence inevitably will lead to your own desensitization.

So, pick up your greatest weapon in this war against pornography and use it—your pen! Keep informed and write to your district attorney, urging enforcement of the state obscenity law. Write to your elected representatives. Write letters to the editor. Write thank-you letters to merchants, newspaper columnists, TV and radio hosts, public officials and others in the public eye who are holding the line against moral decay. You do not have to be a Shakespeare. Just express your feelings in simple terms. One letter, it has been shown, can move mountains, and a mountain of letters can move the direction of an entire country.

A Holocaust survivor once profoundly said, "If you want to know my philosophy about the role of the human being today, it is the story of the just man who comes to Sodom hoping to save the city. So what does he do? He pickets and goes around the city from street to street, from marketplace to marketplace, shouting, 'Men and women, repent. You should know that what you are doing is bad. It will kill you. It will destroy you.' At first they laughed, but then he no longer amuses them as he goes on shouting. One day a child stops him and says, 'Poor stranger, don't you see it's useless?' 'Yes,' the just man replies. 'Then why do you go on?' the child asks. 'I will tell you why,' he says. 'In the beginning, I was convinced that if I were to shout loud enough, I would change them. If I go on shouting, it is because I don't want them to change me.'"

Keep shouting so that you and your children do not unwittingly become victims of behavior modification. And keep praying! The future of America is now up for grabs, and to the victor belongs the next generation of children. Converting your "parlor outrage" into responsible and unrelenting public protest will assure our victory.

6

*"The feminists of the anti-pornography movement
. . . ask women to recognize that they have all
been labeled second-class citizens, all
pornographized."*

Censoring Pornography Would Benefit Women

Nina Burleigh

Many people oppose censoring pornography because they fear censorship would stifle free speech. While such worries must be considered, Nina Burleigh argues in the following viewpoint, she maintains that pornography should be censored in order to protect women. Burleigh contends that pornography reinforces the cultural messages that result in sexual harassment and violence against women. Censoring pornography, she concludes, is one way to decrease these threats. Burleigh is a Washington, D.C.–based freelance writer who specializes in fiction, politics, and women's issues.

As you read, consider the following questions:

1. How is the New Right involved in the anti-pornography movement of radical feminists, according to Burleigh?
2. What does the author mean when she refers to the "split in the self" experienced by women?
3. What is the Cinderella Complex, and how is it an example of the harms caused by pornography, according to Burleigh?

From Nina Burleigh, "The Pornographers," *Arete*, March/April 1989. Reprinted by permission of the author.

To be female and dressed for hot weather on the streets of America's cities is to be bait for lewd words and gestures. It happened to me one summer: "Nice tits," the messenger boy said as he grabbed my breast, then sped off on his bicycle. A minor act in the great scheme of sexual violence, but enough to make me feel like a piece of meat on a supermarket counter.

When a man passes in tight shorts, I don't think of saying, "Nice wad." I wouldn't even think of telling a well-built man passing anonymously on the street that I liked his shoulders, nor can I imagine a fit of passion prompting me to stroke a passing man's backside.

The women's movement has a full agenda even without attacking the difficult problem of the objectification of women's bodies. Most depictions of the movement today define its unifying force as the fight to keep abortion legal. Feminists have been forced to focus on preserving that one great legal victory Fundamental problems such as media and fashion objectification of women and the second-class treatment of women's rights under the law are accorded little attention in mainstream feminist politics.

Fired by Outrage

On the fringes of the women's movement, however, labor anti-pornography feminists, such as Catharine MacKinnon and Andrea Dworkin. These feminists are fired by the outrage women feel when confronted by the reality of the objects their bodies make them in society.

These activists have drafted a model ordinance that carves out a civil remedy for pornography. Potential plaintiffs could be men or women portrayed in pornography or objecting to a piece of pornography that fits the category of subordinating women. Supporters of the law charge that present criminal obscenity laws are not sufficiently enforced and don't help those who are harmed by pornography. The ordinance was approved in Indianapolis and Minneapolis but struck down in the former by the federal courts and in the latter by the mayor. However, it is law in Bellingham, Washington, where it was approved by referendum in November 1988.

In attacking pornography, Dworkin, MacKinnon and others have been accused of attacking free speech. They brush off such objections, arguing that speech is not protected absolutely, that yelling fire for no good reason in a crowded theater is not protected, for example. But more centrally, their premise is that women are harmed by free speech when the scales of justice weigh "obscenity" objections against the First Amendment and come out protecting pornography.

To understand why they can say that, it is necessary to understand how these women view male-female relationships. To

91

them, violence against women, actual or implied, is a fundamental part of female life today. Violence, implied in words, gazes and pictures, inspires violence in deeds such as rape and battery. Implied violence foments fear, and fear silences women. Women portrayed in pornography are the most silenced of all.

The Speech of Exploitation

We have been told that we have an argument here about speech, not about women being hurt. And yet the emblem of that argument is a woman bound and gagged, and we are supposed to believe that that is speech. Who is that speech for? We have women being tortured and we are told that that is somebody's speech? Whose speech is it? It's the speech of a pimp; it is not the speech of a woman. The only words we hear in pornography from women are that women want to be hurt, ask to be hurt, like to be raped, get sexual pleasure from sexual violence; and even when a woman is covered in filth, we are supposed to believe that her speech is that she likes it and she wants more of it.

The reality for women in this society is that pornography creates silence for women. The pornographers silence women. Our bodies are their language. Their speech is made out of our exploitation, our subservience, our injury and our pain.

Andrea Dworkin, testimony before the U.S. Attorney General's Commission on Pornography, January 22, 1986.

Pornography, according to Dworkin, MacKinnon, et al., is sexual harassment, because it glorifies sexual inequality. It is a "dose of domination" for men. They argue that all forms of pornography have the same effect, from the sanitized pictures in *Playboy*, which simply objectify naked women, to the proliferation of material that depicts women bound, gagged, with penises deep in their throats, urinated on, penetrated by objects and animals, physically wounded or tortured.

MacKinnon, a legal scholar who wrote the model anti-porn ordinance, defines the question as a civil rights issue for women: "The second-class status of women" is perpetuated by pornography, because pornography perpetuates "the conviction that, by nature, women are sexually submissive, provoke and enjoy sexual aggression from men, and get sexual pleasure from pain," MacKinnon argues. The anti-pornography ordinance "defines a standard that tells pornographers and their consumers that women are human beings, meaning that when they are hurt, something can be done about it.". . .

Together, Dworkin and MacKinnon have put emotional force

and icy logic into a movement that is absolutist to the core, and which has no patience with the slow pace of change. To them, it's obvious: Women today are oppressed by sexual violence or the threat of it.

Their sense of urgency has not pervaded other feminist groups. The National Organization of Women has resolved that pornography harms women, but it does not support the anti-pornography ordinance. These feminists see the anti-pornography movement as a repudiation of the successes of the women's movement to date.

But MacKinnon can't be written off as a fanatical lawyer from the fringe, because she is responsible for drafting the theory of sexual harassment in the workplace adopted by the U.S. Supreme Court in 1986. She is also a true believer in the theory of sex outlined by Dworkin.

"Law thinks of itself as partial," MacKinnon said recently. "It works to solve marginal problems, not deep, broad, massive structural problems. When you bring up sexual harassment, [judges] still think most sex is not initiated under conditions of inequality. Well, that's an interesting idea, but it's just not that way. So it doesn't even occur to them that by making sexual harassment actionable, they have made actionable the fundamental structure of sexual interaction in society.". . .

The Smut-Stomping Right

It is a mistake to paint the anti-pornography feminists as censors. But the impulse is hard to resist, because the "smut-stomping" nature of the ordinance has found support from zealots of the New Right.

The New Right likes a definition of male-female relationships in which men are inherently aggressive and women inherently victimized. If that's so, say the arch-conservatives, the little woman needs protection, and the domestic sphere is where she belongs.

Surreal political alliances have been forged on this issue. One that stands out is between Dworkin and right-wing preacher Donald Wildmon from Tupelo, Mississippi. Wildmon incorporated some of Dworkin's ideas with his own in 1986 when he served on the eleven-member Attorney General's Commission on Pornography (also known as the Meese Commission). In fact, the commission's finding that pornography is linked to violence was encouraging to the anti-pornography feminists. Another view shared by the New Right and the anti-pornographers is antipathy toward the ACLU [American Civil Liberties Union].

These similarities and alliances worry less radical anti-censorship feminists, who don't buy a Me-Tarzan-You-Jane view of male-female relations.

"The people that would outlaw sexually explicit imagery are

the same people who try to take away women's rights to control their own bodies," says Betty Friedan, who opposes the anti-pornography ordinance. "These women express a righteous rage, but they are dangerous and a disservice to feminism. They are dangerous to constitutional liberties, which are even more important to women than to men."

The fight over constitutional liberties versus freedom from harassment has gotten ugly. Women who have testified about being coerced into pornography have seen their names and addresses subsequently published. In Minneapolis, women were followed and some lost their jobs, according to Therese Stanton, who organized testimony on the anti-pornography ordinance for the Minneapolis City Council.

No information about these dirty tactics reached the general public, the anti-pornography feminists say. Victimized women's testimony is often countered by pornographers and even some journalistic commentators as being merely anecdotal—not scientific enough to be considered proof. "The media keep us invisible," Dworkin complained. "It's all designed to make you think that what we're doing is hateful, that we are in the service of repression."

Because the Minneapolis ordinance was perceived as pro-censorship, it made most journalists wince. During hearings on the ordinance, many newspapers put quotes around the word victim whenever referring to those who claimed to have been hurt by pornography. Even left-leaning writers such as *New Republic*'s Hendrik Hertzberg have trouble being fair to anti-pornography feminists. Hertzberg, for example, admittedly relied on information supplied by *Penthouse's Forum* reporters to depict the bumbling methods of the Attorney General's Commission on Pornography.

Pornographers, particularly *Playboy*, have made much of the connection between mainstream journalists and themselves. In 1979, *Playboy* established the Playboy Foundation First Amendment Awards for journalists, offering cash prizes worth thousands of dollars. Its publicists consistently align the magazine with oft-attacked literature like *The Adventures of Huckleberry Finn*, thereby linking pornography with great art and pornographers with intellectuals.

Women's Silence

MacKinnon argues that in applying the First Amendment to pornography, the application of justice has ironically silenced women. This happens on the level of the pornographic image itself, in which women are depicted as silent bodies or as active bodies enjoying forms of sex that most women don't recognize as enjoyable. The silencing continues in public, when women fear speaking out about their roles in pornography, because of the possible harassment and ridicule. Typical of the difficulties faced by women who speak are the reactions faced by *Deep Throat's* Linda Marchiano, who says she was coerced into pornography. She was smiling in the movie, it's often pointed out.

The Linda Marchiano case is the most egregious example of the ways in which women can be portrayed as "different creatures." To watch a woman with a penis shoved deep into her throat and not be horrified is to believe that the woman's throat is not like one's own. To see a woman tottering on four-inch spike heels and not feel sympathy or amazement is to believe that that woman's feet are not like one's own. These women are split off from men, and all women are split within by the difference between the "alien" and themselves. All women are confronted with this split in the self when confronted with sexual images of women that contradict their familiar selves.

The idea of the split within the self, between the acting body and the silent alien within, is a crucial part of anti-pornography feminist theory. The split within the self, since it's not demonstrable in light of existing research, isn't a concept that stands well with those who fail to see how pornographic actresses are victims. But it is a concept that women can learn to understand. . . .

Realignment of the Liberated with the Victims

What the anti-pornography movement calls for is a reaction to the divide-and-conquer effect that pornography and the silence that goes with it have on women. It asks for the most personal politics. It calls for an alignment of lovers, wives and sweethearts with women who are used, those who are called sluts, whores and bimbos. But this request provokes dissent within the feminist movement. For women to align themselves with the most dominated members of their sex is to admit degrees of their own subordination and victimization. That's a tough task for women who believe they are liberated.

"Liberated" women recognize "the bimbo," the woman with the tractable nature teetering painfully in spike heels, but they don't empathize with her. When women see the standard-issue, male-oriented pornographic pictures, they may speculate on why the subject put her genitalia on display. But they don't align themselves with her.

There are deep-seated cultural and psychological reasons why women "collaborate" in their subordination. The second-class status that comes with womanhood and poverty are two of the most obvious reasons. The anti-pornography activists go further, saying most prostitutes and pornography models were victims of rape or incest as young women or girls.

Women victims of abuse, including the abuse that goes with

participating in pornography and prostitution, are extreme examples of a psychology of passivity known as the Cinderella Complex, identified by New York psychologist and author Rita Freedman. Passivity gives women power in a male-dominated society. Women rely on make-up and debilitating props like high heels to enhance their passive image. Even comprehending that, it is difficult to sympathize with women who testified at the Attorney General's Pornography Commission clad in sexy blouses and spike heels, as *Playboy*'s reporter on the scene was quick to describe. At a New York conference on trafficking women, former prostitutes and pornographic actresses "spoke out" about their experiences. One, a former pornographic model, wore spike heels and make-up while describing how she worked in pornographic films for nine months to support herself and her boyfriend. A former prostitute showed up at the podium in a clingy white dress, flawlessly made up and wearing high heels. These women—while they profess to have a "raised consciousness"—still rely on the passive props that were so important to their former trades.

"Victims"

Society frequently blames victims for their problems. William Ryan, in *Blaming the Victim*, outlined the phenomenon. Deep down, many believe there must be something wrong with people who have bad things, particularly sexually bad things, happen to them. Hence, it is understandable that the media often reacts by putting quotation marks around sexual "victims."

For [contemporary] women, dressed for success, making the ego-shattering leap from "victor" to "victim" is perhaps too much to ask. As the messenger boy snickered and sped away from me on the street, I vaguely recognized—for a split second—that I was a victim. I soon forgot that feeling, puffed strong with righteous rage. I'm a career-oriented, independent woman, after all. I'm no prey, no martyr, no streetwalker, no battered wife, no incest victim, no sex object.

Only months later did I wonder who told that young man he could touch me and call out "nice tits." The feminists of the anti-pornography movement have an appealingly pure and simple answer. They ask women to recognize that they have all been labeled second-class citizens, all pornographized, whether they wear make-up or not, whether they are lawyers or prostitutes. They would say these men carry to women the message of the pornographers whose *D-Cup* and *Screw* and *Playboy* and *Hustler* objectify and sexualize women's bodies. . . .

As a writer, it is a personal insult to me that the great idea behind the free speech clause has been used to protect a $10 billion industry whose main product depicts women as brainless bedroom kittens at best, and at worst victims of bestial crimes. As a writer, it is easy for me to see the difference between the subjugation of women in a book like William Faulkner's *Sanctuary*, once ruled obscene for its corn cob rape, and in a corn cob rape depicted graphically in a pornographic video. When one finishes *Sanctuary*, one tastes the evil of violence. In the videotape, only the lust of the victimizer, free of any moral context, is conveyed.

The many haters of beauty and thought in this country could employ the anti-pornography ordinance to attack books like *Sanctuary*. The feminists' rage at violence against women has filtered into and tainted their ordinance. But their urgency is no less valid, because at the end of the 20th century, women remain trapped in a grid of leers and remarks, sexualized at every turn even as they go to work alongside men.

7

"Censorship is antithetical to the fight for women's rights."

Censoring Pornography Would Not Benefit Women

Nadine Strossen

In the following viewpoint, Nadine Strossen maintains that censorship of pornography does nothing to protect women from sexual harassment or violence. Women have the right to view and participate in pornography, Strossen argues, and censoring such materials only robs women of the right to make their own choices. Strossen is a professor of constitutional law at New York Law School and president of the American Civil Liberties Union. She is the author of the book *Defending Pornography: Free Speech, Sex, and the Fight for Women's Rights*, from which this viewpoint is adapted.

As you read, consider the following questions:

1. How did the women's liberation movement free women sexually, according to Strossen?
2. Why does Strossen call the anti-pornography feminists' views "Victorian"?
3. How has the fight between anti-pornography and anti-censorship feminists harmed feminism, in the author's opinion?

Excerpted from Nadine Strossen, "The Perils of Pornophobia," *Humanist*, May/June 1995. Reprinted by permission of the author.

In 1992, in response to a complaint, officials at Pennsylvania State University unceremoniously removed Francisco de Goya's masterpiece, *The Nude Maja*, from a classroom wall. The complaint had not been lodged by Jesse Helms or some irate member of the Christian Coalition. Instead, the complainant was a feminist English professor who protested that the eighteenth-century painting of a recumbent nude woman made her and her female students "uncomfortable."

This was not an isolated incident. At the University of Arizona at Tucson, feminist students physically attacked a graduate student's exhibit of photographic self-portraits. Why? The artist had photographed *herself* in her *underwear*. And at the University of Michigan Law School, feminist students who had organized a conference on "Prostitution: From Academia to Activism" removed a feminist-curated art exhibition held in conjunction with the conference. Their reason? Conference speakers had complained that a composite videotape containing interviews of working prostitutes was "pornographic" and therefore unacceptable.

What is wrong with this picture? Where have they come from—these feminists who behave like religious conservatives, who censor works of art because they deal with sexual themes? Have not feminists long known that censorship is a dangerous weapon which, if permitted, would inevitably be turned against them? Certainly that was the irrefutable lesson of the early women's rights movement, when Margaret Sanger, Mary Ware Dennett, and other activists were arrested, charged with "obscenity," and prosecuted for distributing educational pamphlets about sex and birth control. Theirs was a struggle for freedom of sexual expression and full gender equality, which they understood to be mutually reinforcing.

The Liberation of Female Sexuality

Theirs was also a lesson well understood by the second wave of feminism in the 1970s, when writers such as Germaine Greer, Betty Friedan, and Betty Dodson boldly asserted that women had the right to be free from discrimination not only in the workplace and in the classroom but in the bedroom as well. Freedom from limiting, conventional stereotypes concerning female sexuality was an essential aspect of what we then called "women's liberation." Women should not be seen as victims in their sexual relations with men but as equally assertive partners, just as capable of experiencing sexual pleasure.

But it is a lesson that, alas, many feminists have now forgotten. Today, an increasingly influential feminist pro-censorship movement threatens to impair the very women's rights movement it professes to serve. Led by law professor Catharine MacKinnon and writer Andrea Dworkin, this faction of the feminist movement maintains that sexually oriented *expression*—not sex-segregated labor markets, sexist concepts of marriage and family, or pent-up rage—is the preeminent cause of discrimination and violence against women. Their solution is seemingly simple: suppress all "pornography."

Censorship, however, is never a simple matter. First, the offense must be described. And how does one define something so infinitely variable, so deeply personal, so uniquely individualized as the image, the word, and the fantasy that cause sexual arousal? For decades, the U.S. Supreme Court has engaged in a Sisyphean struggle to craft a definition of *obscenity* that the lower courts can apply with some fairness and consistency. Their dilemma was best summed up in former Justice Potter Stewart's now famous statement: "I shall not today attempt further to define [obscenity]; and perhaps I could never succeed in intelligibly doing so. But I know it when I see it."

The Appeal of Image-Blaming

As a proposal for life's improvement, image-blaming has several charms to its advantage. It offers the boost of activism. Sexual imagery is visible, tinged with the illicit, and far easier to expunge than deeply rooted injustices. Well-meaning citizens believe they can fight it, beat it, and win. Feminists are exhausted fighting a sexist economy and politics and sexual violence. Most Americans are at a loss in a difficult economy and in the face of rapid changes in gender, family, and race relations. The "decency" movements are a boon to those who want to feel they control their lives. In this, these movements have the same appeal as the fantasies they assail. They provide a frightening but beatable monster and the pledge of a happy ending. As long as life is insecure, this promise will have a market. Like monster movies and pornography, image-blaming is a fantasy that sells.

Marcia Pally, *SIECUS Report*, October/November 1994.

The censorious feminists are not so modest as Justice Stewart. They have fashioned an elaborate definition of *pornography* that encompasses vastly more material than does the currently recognized law of *obscenity*. As set out in their model law (which has been considered in more than a dozen jurisdictions in the United States and overseas, and which has been substantially adopted in Canada), pornography is "the sexually explicit subordination of women through pictures and/or words." The model law lists eight different criteria that attempt to illustrate their concept of "subordination," such as depictions in which "women are presented in postures or positions of sexual submission, servility, or display" or "women are presented in scenarios of degradation, humiliation, injury, torture . . . in a context that makes these conditions sexual." This linguistic driftnet can ensnare anything from religious imagery and documentary footage about the mass rapes in the Balkans to self-help books about women's health. Indeed, the Boston Women's Health Book Collective, publisher of the now-classic book on women's health and sexuality, *Our Bodies, Ourselves*, actively campaigned against the MacKinnon-Dworkin model law when it was proposed in Cambridge, Massachusetts, in 1985, recognizing that the book's explicit text and pictures could be targeted as pornographic under the law.

Although the "MacDworkinite" approach to pornography has an intuitive appeal to many feminists, it is itself based on subordinating and demeaning stereotypes about women. Central to the pornophobic feminists—and to many traditional conservatives and right-wing fundamentalists, as well—is the notion that sex is inherently degrading to women (although not to men). Not just sexual expression but sex itself—even consensual, nonviolent sex—is an evil from which women, like children, must be protected.

MacKinnon puts it this way: "Compare victims' reports of rape with women's reports of sex. They look a lot alike. . . . The major distinction between intercourse (normal) and rape (abnormal) is that the normal happens so often that one can not get anyone to see anything wrong with it." And from Dworkin: "Intercourse remains a means or the means of physiologically making a woman inferior." Given society's pervasive sexism, she believes, women cannot freely consent to sexual relations with men; those who do consent are, in Dworkin's words, "collaborators . . . experiencing pleasure in their own inferiority."

Victorian Notions

These ideas are hardly radical. Rather, they are a reincarnation of disempowering puritanical, Victorian notions that feminists have long tried to consign to the dustbin of history: woman as sexual victim; man as voracious satyr. The MacDworkinite approach to sexual expression is a throwback to the archaic stereotypes that formed the basis for nineteenth-century laws which prohibited "vulgar" or sexually suggestive language from being used in the presence of women and girls.

In those days, women were barred from practicing law and serving as jurors lest they be exposed to such language. Such "protective" laws have historically functioned to bar women from full legal equality. Paternalism always leads to exclusion, discrimination, and the loss of freedom and autonomy. And in its most extreme form, it leads to purdah, in which women are completely shrouded from public view.

The pro-censorship feminists are not fighting alone. Although they try to distance themselves from such traditional "family-values" conservatives as Jesse Helms, Phyllis Schlafly, and Donald Wildmon, who are less interested in protecting women than in preserving male dominance, a common hatred of sexual expression and fondness for censorship unite the two camps. For example, the Indianapolis City Council adopted the MacKinnon-Dworkin model law in 1984 thanks to the hard work of former council member Beulah Coughenour, a leader of the Indiana Stop ERA movement. (Federal courts later declared the law unconstitutional.) And when Phyllis Schlafly's Eagle Forum and Beverly LaHaye's Concerned Women for America launched their "Enough Is Enough" anti-pornography campaign, they trumpeted the words of Andrea Dworkin in promotional materials.

This mutually reinforcing relationship does a serious disservice to the fight for women's equality. It lends credibility to and strengthens the right wing and its anti-feminist, anti-choice, homophobic agenda. This is particularly damaging in light of the growing influence of the religious right in the Republican Party and the 1994 Republican sweep of both Congress and many state governments. If anyone doubts that the newly empowered GOP intends to forge ahead with anti-woman agendas, they need only read the party's "Contract with America" which, among other things, reintroduces the recently repealed "gag rule" forbidding government-funded family-planning clinics from even discussing abortion with their patients. . . .

Censorship Backfires

There *is* mounting evidence, however, that MacDworkinite-type laws will be used against the very people they are supposed to protect—namely, women. In 1992, for example, the Canadian Supreme Court incorporated the MacKinnon-Dworkin concept of pornography into Canadian obscenity law. Since that ruling, in *Butler v. The Queen*—which MacKinnon enthusiastically hailed as "a stunning victory for women"—well over half of all feminist bookstores in Canada have had materials confiscated or detained by customs. According to the *Feminist Bookstore News*, a Canadian publication, "The *Butler* decision has been used . . . only to seize lesbian, gay, and feminist material."

Ironically but predictably, one of the victims of Canada's new law is Andrea Dworkin herself. Two of her books, *Pornography: Men Possessing Women* and *Women Hating*, were seized, customs officials said, because they "illegally eroticized pain and bondage." Like the MacKinnon-Dworkin model law, the *Butler* decision makes no exceptions for material that is part of a feminist critique of pornography or other feminist presentation. And this inevitably overbroad sweep is precisely why censorship is antithetical to the fight for women's rights.

The pornophobia that grips MacKinnon, Dworkin, and their followers has had further counterproductive impacts on the fight for women's rights. Censorship factionalism within the feminist movement has led to an enormously wasteful diversion of energy from the real cause of and solutions to the ongoing problems of discrimination and violence against women. Moreover, the "porn-made-me-do-it" defense, whereby convicted rapists cite MacKinnon and Dworkin in seeking to reduce their sentences, actually impedes the aggressive enforcement of criminal laws against sexual violence.

A return to the basic principles of women's liberation would put the feminist movement back on course. We women are entitled to freedom of expression—to read, think, speak, sing, write, paint, dance, dream, photograph, film, and fantasize as we wish. We are also entitled to our dignity, autonomy, and equality. Fortunately, we can—and will—have both.

Periodical Bibliography

The following articles have been selected to supplement the diverse views presented in this chapter. Addresses are provided for periodicals not indexed in the *Readers' Guide to Periodical Literature*, the *Alternative Press Index*, or the *Social Sciences Index*.

Amy Adler	"Buttoning Up Porn," *Nation*, October 16, 1995.
Denise Caruso	"Always a New Exception, Always a New Reason," *New York Times*, May 1, 1995.
Christianity Today	"Making Porn Pay," April 27, 1992.
Stuart Elliott	"Will Calvin Klein's Retreat Redraw the Lines of Taste?" *New York Times*, August 29, 1995.
Marjorie Garber	"Maximum Exposure," *New York Times*, December 4, 1993.
Stephanie Gutmann	"Waging War on Sex Crimes and Videotape," *Insight*, May 3, 1993. Available from 3600 New York Ave. NE, Washington, DC 20002.
Wray Herbert	"Is Porn Un-American? Cincinnati Wonders How Far to Go in Its Campaign Against Smut," *U.S. News & World Report*, July 3, 1995.
Mark Y. Herring	"Cybersex," *St. Croix Review*, October 1995. Available from PO Box 244, Stillwater, MN 55082.
Patricia Lefevere	"The Thorny Debate over Art vs. Pornography," *National Catholic Reporter*, February 17, 1995. Available from PO Box 281, Kansas City, MO 64141.
Susan Monaco	"When Advertising Is Obscene," *Sojourners*, November/December 1995.
Eugene Narrett	"Does Calvin Klein Work Out? A Case for Censorship," *Culture Wars*, January 1996. Available from 206 Marquette Ave., South Bend, IN 46617.
New York Times	"Is Magazine Smut or Satire? Court to Decide," November 26, 1995.
Ernest van den Haag	"Thinking About Rape," *American Spectator*, April 1992.

3

Should Pornography on the Internet Be Regulated?

Pornography

Chapter Preface

The Internet, a worldwide network of computers and databases, has evolved rapidly in recent years. Enormous amounts of information are now available on the Internet via a typical home computer. Much of the material is educational, informative, or entertaining. However, some of it is pornographic—from simple photos of nude people to photos and graphic descriptions of torture and other forms of brutality.

The existence of pornography on the Internet has sparked a debate over whether cyberspace should be regulated. The Internet was largely unregulated until February 1996, when the Telecommunications Act of 1996 was enacted. One portion of that act, the Communications Decency Act (CDA), made it illegal to make indecent material accessible to minors on the Internet. The law required providers of Internet access to make good-faith efforts to restrict access to indecent materials by requiring users to provide a verified credit card account number or a password.

Advocates believe that the CDA is necessary to ensure that children are not exposed to sexually explicit material when using their home computers. Nebraska senator James Exon, who sponsored the Senate version of the CDA, says, "We are taking the antismut and antipornography laws that have long been in place with the telephone and the mails and applying them to the information superhighway. I want to make the information superhighway as safe as possible for kids."

Opponents of the CDA argue that restricting the Internet threatens freedom of speech. The CDA, says Marc Rotenberg of the Electronic Privacy Information Center, is "government censorship. The First Amendment shouldn't end where the Internet begins." In June of 1996, a special federal court panel drew a similar conclusion. It barred the government from enforcing the CDA, stating, "As the most participatory form of mass speech yet developed, the Internet deserves the highest protection from governmental intrusion."

The battle over the CDA reveals how difficult it can be to balance the need to protect society from potential harms while simultaneously ensuring the public's First Amendment rights. The viewpoints in the following chapter, written prior to the passage of the CDA, present cogent arguments for and against government censorship of pornography on the Internet.

"The 'information superhighway' must be designed with protections for children. Pornographers cannot and will not police themselves."

Internet Pornography Should Be Censored

Deen Kaplan

Deen Kaplan is the president of public policy for the National Coalition Against Pornography (N-CAP), a national organization that works to pass laws censoring pornography. In the following viewpoint, Kaplan outlines the types of pornography that are available on the Internet. He argues that such materials lead some people to commit violent sexual crimes against women and children. Kaplan concludes that pornography on the Internet must be censored to protect society.

As you read, consider the following questions:

1. What technological advances have been exploited by pornographers, according to Kaplan?
2. Why is interactive pornography especially harmful, in the author's opinion?
3. What steps does Kaplan suggest would help regulate Internet pornography?

From Deen Kaplan, "Pornography and Cyberspace: The Final Frontier," *Family Voice*, August 1994. Reprinted by permission of Concerned Women for America.

107

Parents have reason to be alarmed—across America the pornography industry is now invading our children's bedrooms through home computers. "Cybersex" presents a sobering reality, but an essential one for us to understand if we are to win the war against this new form of abuse.

Since its inception, the pornography industry has operated with two primary business goals. First, remove as much of the social stigma as possible from consuming pornography. Second, seek to use every advance in technology to make purchasing and consuming pornography easier.

Abusive pornography used in the privacy of one's home, with little social stigma, is no less dangerous than purchasing and using the same material in public. The content of the material itself, which has grown ever worse, is harmful. Pornography plays a significant role in sexual violence against women, child abuse, sexual harassment, destroyed marriages, sexually transmitted diseases and warped attitudes among many men towards women.

In the 1980s, there were a number of technological advances, each carefully exploited by pornographers. The advent of both the home VCR and the lack of law enforcement against illegal pornography helped the industry take off. Sales figures skyrocketed. A curious customer no longer had to travel to the worst part of town to enter a disgusting peep show to get his material—he could travel to the "respectable" mom-and-pop video store down the street and find the same materials. Many men bought their first VCR just to watch pornography.

Finally, the first personal computers (PCs) were created in the early 80s. In the beginning, PCs weren't powerful enough to serve as a vehicle for pornography, but that has radically changed in the last few years. And computer technology developments will continue to shape how the pornography industry markets its products over the next decade.

The Future of High-Tech Porn

Where are we headed? First, computers and digital technology in the future will drive many of the new channels of distribution. This has already begun. Many computer-based bulletin board services (BBS) offer the equivalent of an entire pornographic bookstore "online." Hard-core pictures are scanned into computers and then made available to any home computer owner through the telephone line and an inexpensive device called a modem.

The pictures downloaded from these computers are as clear and vivid as those in magazines and videos. Yet few of these distributors ever check the age of those who sign on to their systems. Children, who are usually the computer experts in the family, have access to these materials from the computer in their bedrooms. More and more, parents are discovering their child has gotten dozens of pornographic pictures from a local or national computer BBS.

Finding Porn on the Internet

The entire spectrum of pornographic material is available on computer networks including images of soft-core nudity, hard-core sex acts, anal sex, bestiality, bondage & dominion, sado-masochism (including actual torture and mutilation, usually of women, for sexual pleasure), scatological acts (defecating and urinating, usually on women, for sexual pleasure), fetishes, and child pornography. Additionally, there is textual pornography including detailed text stories of the rape, mutilation, and torture of women, sexual abuse of children, graphic incest, etc.

Virtually anyone with an account or access to the Internet can access pornography. Once "on-line" there are no truly effective safety measures to prevent children from accessing all of the pornography described above. This unlimited access to pornography, with no accurate, enforceable age check and no verification procedures, has never occurred in the print, broadcast, satellite or cable media before. Cyberspace is currently the free speech absolutist's dream world.

Family Research Council, *In Focus*, November 8, 1995.

Second, pornographers are beginning to exploit interactive computer technology. Multimedia computers enable consumers to purchase storage disks known as CD-ROMs where the consumer can interact with a moving, speaking picture of a woman on the screen. He can tie her up or tell her to perform various acts on the screen for him. This interaction has dire consequences. It moves the pornography addict quickly from a passive observer to a full participant (making it more likely he will act out the same fantasies on real people in our neighborhoods). Dozens of young boys, after listening to hours of Dial-A-Porn in the early 80s, went out and abused young girls in exactly the way described to them over the phone. Now, the child has a moving picture on the computer to further stimulate his fantasy.

Third, the digital technology so prevalent in computers will soon transform the media we receive in our homes. Many citizens have read recent news accounts of televisions with 500 channels and thousands of choices. Unless action is taken now, some of these channels will offer explicit pornography to homes all across America.

Last, computers have become the tool of choice for child molesters and pedophiles. Pedophiles use personal computers to store and trade images of abused children, to seduce children through "chat" conferences on computer BBS systems and to lessen their risk of capture by law enforcement. International child pornography rings now use computers to distribute their images of children throughout the world.

While this picture is sobering, the battle is by no means lost! We can't allow pornographers to use positive technological progress for evil purposes. Massive legislative, legal and educational efforts are needed. A key first step is to let your congressman know that the "information superhighway" must be designed with protections for children. Pornographers cannot and will not police themselves.

Pornographers traffic the abuse of women and children for profit. They must be stopped now!

"One man's porn is another man's magazine illustration—a fact that should make Congress hesitate before it tries to restrict . . . pornography in cyberspace."

Internet Pornography Should Not Be Censored

John Corry

Many commentators contend that pornography is readily available on the Internet and that regulations are needed to prevent children from being exposed to obscene words and images. In the following viewpoint, John Corry argues that these claims are exaggerated. He insists that the amount of pornography on the Internet is minimal and that such material is difficult to locate and access. He maintains that censoring the Internet would pose a threat to free speech that would far exceed any imagined harm that could come from Internet pornography. Corry, a former *New York Times* media critic, is the author of the book *My Times: Adventures in the News Trade*.

As you read, consider the following questions:

1. Corry quotes U.S. senator Orrin Hatch as saying that the entire issue of censoring Internet pornography is a "game." Explain the senator's point.
2. According to the Carnegie Mellon study cited by the author, what percentage of messages on the Internet were associated with newsgroups that distributed pornography?
3. Why is it difficult for children to gain access to pornography on the Internet, according to Corry?

From John Corry, "Salty V-Chips," *American Spectator*, September 1995. Copyright by The American Spectator. Reprinted with permission.

It was not supposed to happen. Conservatives are now calling for government censorship, a notion that until recently was advocated only by liberals. When Congress was controlled by Democrats, it was full of proposals to stifle free speech. Under the Republicans, things were supposed to get better. But in fact they are not, and otherwise sensible people are doing foolish things. Many flowers of the Republican Party, along with their allies in the Christian Coalition, are joining with discredited liberals, radical feminists, and an assortment of social engineers to undermine the First Amendment with some absolutely harebrained proposals.

The history here is complicated, stretching back to the early days of television, but it is connected by a single idea: that bureaucrats know what is best for us. In June 1995 the Senate voted to require manufacturers to install computer chips—the so-called V-chips—into new television sets; the chips would allow parents to lock out programs that presumably are unsuitable for children. In theory, broadcasters would transmit a signal with each program, indicating whether it contained violent or sexual content. The V-chip would then be programmed so that it blocked all broadcasts that a rating code deemed offensive. The broadcasters would be given a year to develop the rating code by themselves, and if they did not, the Senate said, the federal government would appoint a committee to do it for them. However, there is not the slightest chance that broadcasters will, or can, develop a uniform rating code. There are more than 11 million hours of television programming each year, and it is absurd to think that broadcasters could devise a ratings system that would apply to all of them. Under the circumstances, the government committee would be sure to step in. Bureaucrats would apply their own standards to determine what is appropriate for the rest of us to see.

Enthusiasm for the V-chip was swept along by the desire to regulate violence on television, long a passion of congressional liberals, although always resisted in the past by conservatives.

Peeking at Dirty Pictures

Fearful, however, that a vote against the V-chip might be interpreted as a vote against family values, many conservatives reversed their positions. Then, the day after they struck out at violence, they decided to go all out against smut. James Exon, the Nebraska Democrat, turned up on the Senate floor with a folder full of dirty pictures that his staff had copied off the Internet. Actually, there has been porn on the Internet for a long time, and some of its distributors have been imprisoned for violating anti-obscenity laws. Senators, though, professed shock when they peeked inside Exon's folder—it had a red label on it that said, "Caution"—and decided they had to do more, especially since a national audience was watching on C-Span. They voted 84-16 to impose criminal penalties on anyone who intentionally annoys or bothers anyone else with an "obscene, lewd, lascivious, filthy or indecent" comment, request, or suggestion over a computer network. This means you may be prosecuted for using e-mail to tell your brother-in-law, say, that something he did has left you "pissed off."

Exchanging Liberty for Safety

People who display great common sense in all other matters, and who fervently believe in the constitutional protections for privacy and free speech and freedom of assembly, crumple when someone from law enforcement says: "There are child pornographers . . . on the net. Don't you think we should use whatever means possible to stop them?"

But the argument "we're doing this for your own good" is a slippery slope when applied to free speech. Perverts and criminals will always be with us. Once they are stopped (always temporarily, if at all), who is next to be watched? As Benjamin Franklin said, "They who can give up essential liberty to obtain a little temporary safety deserve neither liberty nor safety."

The decisions we make today will be ones we live with for a very long time. If we want our Constitution to remain intact through today's turbulent times, we can't afford to demonize the Internet, or any other medium of human communication.

Denise Caruso, *New York Times*, May 1, 1995.

"It's kind of a game, to see who can be the most against pornography and obscenity," Orrin Hatch said sourly. "It's a political exercise, and I'm against it." Hatch was one of the few conservatives who stood firm against government regulation, and he was right about it being a game. *Time* magazine soon came out with a wide-eyed, open-mouthed, apparently horrified, but otherwise angelic little blue-eyed boy on its cover. He was working at his computer, and supposedly had just seen something unspeakable on the screen. "Cyberporn," the headline read, and underneath that: "Exclusive: A new study shows just how pervasive and wild it really is."

In fact, the new study was not entirely exclusive, and it did not really show how pervasive or wild cyberporn really is. If you paid close attention, it might even have suggested the opposite. The study, conducted at Carnegie Mellon University, found that "83.5 percent of all images posted on the Usenet are pornographic." The finding, as reported by *Time*, was much noted. Charles Grassley cited it when he held a copy of the magazine aloft in the Senate, and defended his support for the Exon bill; Ralph Reed, the director of the Christian Coalition, used it when he argued on television for government action. Further down in its story, though, *Time* had noted another Carnegie Mellon finding: that pornographic image files represented only 3 percent of the traffic on the Usenet bulletin boards, called newsgroups, while the Usenet represented only 11.5 percent of the traffic on Internet. This meant that less than one-half of 1 percent—or 3 percent of 11.5 percent—of all the messages on Internet were associated with the newsgroups that peddled pornographic pictures. Moreover, some of these messages were surely benign. Anti-porn hunters, for example, often post messages on these so-called adult bulletin boards. "You will all burn in hell" is one of their favorites.

Thus the 83.5 percent figure seemed to melt away. It was hard to tell what, if anything, it meant. The principal Carnegie Mellon researcher, an undergraduate in electrical engineering, had gathered most of his data from the adult bulletin boards. These adult bulletin boards charge fees, accept credit cards, and usually demand proof of age—a driver's license will do—before they let you order anything shocking. The little boy on *Time*'s cover would have had to steal his father's driver's license, Xerox it, scan it into the Internet, send a credit card number, and then find a way of explaining to his parents why they were getting the bill. Moreover, while there are something like 15,000 bulletin boards, or newsgroups, on Usenet, most do not store and transmit digitized images; they disperse words and not pictures. The Carnegie Mellon researchers had found most of the pornographic images exactly where they might be expected to find them. It was as if they had walked into an adult bookstore in a seedy neighborhood, and ignored the public library a few blocks away.

But, as Orrin Hatch said, the game was to show who would stand most firmly against pornography. Competition was setting in. *Time* offered "Nightline" exclusive coverage of its report. "Nightline" accepted, and opened its program with Marty Rimm, who had led the Carnegie Mellon research team. "Pedophilia, bestiality, vaginal and rectal fisting, sadomasochism," he intoned, and then came the voice of Ted Koppel: "Now, it's the kind of material you and your kids can see with just the click of a button."

Difficult to Find

Nonetheless, you do not see that material with just the click of a button. Cyberspace is more impenetrable than that, a point nicely illustrated later that week on "Crossfire." An agitated John Sununu, arguing with Nadine Strossen, the president of the American Civil Liberties Union, said you needed only "a few clicks" to pull up filthy material. Then he said that Michael Kinsley, presumably experimenting, had done it "with five clicks the other night." Later, still arguing with Strossen, Sununu raised this to "half a dozen clicks," whereupon Kinsley finally interrupted. All he had managed to pull up, he said, was a *Playboy* centerfold.

As filthy material, however, this wasn't much, no matter what Sununu thought. One man's porn is another man's magazine illustration—a fact that should make Congress hesitate before it tries to restrict either violence on television or pornography in cyberspace. . . .

There is no telling where the censorious zeal may strike next. Passions are rising, and some of them are unhealthy. Ralph Reed grew so testy on "Crossfire" that he accused Nadine Strossen of advocating "bestiality." The ACLU president, of course, had done no such thing, and it may be that Reed was angry because only minutes before he had been made to look foolish and perhaps even sinister. Michael Kinsley had asked him whether he wanted to keep smut away from adults as well as from children. Reed gave an ambiguous answer, and so Kinsley asked him again. In fact, he repeated the question three times, but Reed remained ambiguous.

One had a vision of speech codes or worse. The director of the Christian Coalition seemed to be lining up with Catharine MacKinnon. The radical feminist law professor had praised the Carnegie Mellon study. "The question pornography poses in cyberspace," she wrote in the *Georgetown Law Journal*, "is the same one it poses everywhere else: whether anything will be done about it." MacKinnon, as always, called for censorship. Reed appeared to want that, too. Strossen, however, has pointed out that MacKinnon and her followers are not only anti-pornography; they are anti-sex as well. These are the twin poles in the totalitarian thinking of commissars and gauleiters. The ACLU seems to be taking a sounder position here than the Christian Coalition.

"*Parents can buy some sophisticated software to block children's access to questionable material.*"

Parents Can Protect Children from Internet Pornography

Steven Levy

Some policy makers have advocated legal measures designed to protect children from sexual content on the Internet. In the following viewpoint, Steven Levy suggests that censoring Internet pornography through government legislation could impede communication on the Internet and slow the advance of technological progress. Instead, Levy advises parents to use new software programs and to explain honestly to their children the harmful nature of Internet pornography. Levy is a writer and contributing editor for *Newsweek* magazine.

As you read, consider the following questions:

1. What are some of the dangers children face from Internet pornography, according to the author?
2. How can software programs prevent children from viewing pornography on the Internet, according to Levy?
3. What is Levy's final conclusion about the nature of raising children?

When the annals of cyberspace are uploaded for future generations, digital historians will undoubtedly include a July 1995 scene from the Senate chamber: Nebraska Democrat James Exon brandishing a thin binder now known as the blue book. Inside were images snatched from the shadows and thrust into the center of public discourse. Women bound and being burned by cigarettes. Pierced with swords. Having sex with a German shepherd. As Exon puts it, images that are "repulsive and far off base." Images from the Net.

Exon compiled his blue book to persuade his Senate colleagues to pass his Communications Decency Act. Partially moved by a private showing in the Senate cloakroom, they did so, overwhelmingly. The act, which places strict limits on all speech in computer networks [was signed into law as part of the Telecommunications Bill of 1996]. . . . Even the most vehement of the Internet's defenders now face a real problem: how to maintain free speech when well-chronicled excesses give the impression that much of cyberspace is a cesspool.

Indeed, most of the dispatches from the electronic world these days seem to dwell on the dark side. The most prevalent type of anecdote involves someone like Susan Tilghman, a medical doctor in Fairfax, Va. She hooked the family computer to America Online (AOL). Her sons, 12 and 15 years old, enjoyed it so much that she and her husband sought to find out why. Clicking on files their boys had read, the astonished parents found "pornographic pictures in full color," says Tilghman. "We were horrified." She pulled the modem plug immediately.

Then there are the actual busts of online pornographic rings. Just as in the physical world, traffic in obscene material is illegal in cyberspace, and authorities are beginning to prosecute zealously. . . .

Most disturbing of all are the tales of sexual predators using the Internet and commercial online services to spirit children away from their keyboards. Until now parents have believed that no physical harm could possibly result when their progeny were huddled safely in the bedroom or den, tapping on the family computer. But then came news of cases like the 13-year-old Kentucky girl found in Los Angeles after supposedly being lured by a grown-up cyberpal.

Parental Panic

These reports have triggered a sort of parental panic about cyberspace. Parents are rightfully confused, faced with hard choices about whether to expose their children to the alleged benefits of cyberspace when carnal pitfalls lie ahead. As our culture moves unrelentingly toward the digital realm, some questions—and answers—are finally coming into focus.

How much sex is there in cyberspace? A lot. Brian Reid, director of the Network Systems Laboratory at Digital Equipment Corp., reports that one of the most popular of the thousands of Usenet discussion groups is the "alt.sex" group. He estimates that on a monthly basis between 180,000 and 500,000 users drop in. A glance at some World Wide Web sites shows that while the digital home of the Smithsonian Institution took seven weeks to gather 1.9 million visits, or "hits," Playboy's electronic headquarters received 4.7 million hits in a seven-day period.

And the *Georgetown Law Journal* released a survey headed by Marty Rimm, a 30-year-old researcher at Carnegie Mellon University. In his paper, "Marketing Pornography on the Information Superhighway," Rimm concentrated mostly on adults-only bulletin boards (the equivalent of X-rated bookshops). He provides solid evidence that there's loads of hard-core stuff in cyberspace. Rimm wrote a computer program to analyze descriptions of 917,410 dirty pictures (he examined about 10,000 actual images, to check the reliability of the descriptions). His conclusion: "I think there's almost no question that we're seeing an unprecedented availability and demand of material like sadomasochism, bestiality, vaginal and rectal fisting, eroticized urination . . . and pedophilia."

How easy is it to avoid the sexual material? Donna Rice Hughes (yes, *that* Donna Rice), spokesperson for an anti-pornography group called Enough Is Enough!, claims that "children are going online innocently and naively running across material that's illegal even for adults." But the way the Internet works, that sort of stuff doesn't tend to pop up uninvited. "When you watch TV it comes right at you," says Donna Hoffman, associate professor of business at Vanderbilt University. "But on the Internet, you're in an environment with 30 million channels. It's up to you to decide where to go. You don't have to download the images on alt.sex.binaries."

Groups with "binaries" are the picture files, the ones containing the most shocking images. To find them, one needs a good sense of digital direction. Depending on the software you have, you may need a mastery of some codes in the notoriously arcane Unix computer language, or it can involve a few well-chosen clicks of the mouse. In any case, there's no way you get that stuff by accident.

How to Protect Kids

Kids are very hungry to view sexual materials, and left to their own devices they will find that the Internet provides them with an unprecedented bonanza. In predigital days, getting one's hands on hot pictures required running an often impenetrable gantlet of drugstore clerks and newsstand operators, and

118

finding really hard-core material was out of the question. Not so with the Net. Frank Moretti, associate headmaster of the Dalton School in New York City, which offers Internet access beginning in junior high, thinks that we can deal with that. "There's a candy store around the corner from our school that has just about every kind of pornographic image," he says. "The challenge is to help our children use self-discipline."

Is the Internet a haven for predators? After years of online activity, "there have been about a dozen high-profile cases," says Ernie Allen, president of the Arlington, Va.–based National Center for Missing and Exploited Children. "It's not a huge number, but it does indicate that there are risks. But there are risks in everything a child does. Our concern is the nature of the technology. It creates a false sense of security."

"CRUISE THE INFORMATION SUPERHIGHWAY ALL YOU WANT... BUT IF I CATCH YOU IN ANY BACK ALLEYS, UNDERPASSES OR ON THE SUNSET STRIP, YOU'LL LOSE YOUR DRIVERS LICENSE!"

Heller, for the *Green Bay Press-Gazette*. Reprinted with permission.

What parents should warn kids about is the classic scenario described by Detective Bill Dworn, head of the Sexually Exploited Child Unit of the Los Angeles Police Department: "The pervert can get on any bulletin board and chat with kids all night long. He lies about his age and makes friends. As soon as he can get a telephone number or address, he's likely to look up the kid and molest him or her." In real life, this hardly ever happens. Most online services have policies to monitor chat rooms, particularly those designated as "kids-only." No guarantees, but not many kidnappers.

And if the child is propositioned? "It happens, but it's less upsetting if a child is prepared for it," says Sherry Turkle, an MIT professor whose book, *Life on the Screen*, includes data about the experiences of nearly 300 kids on the Net. "Better to warn the child and instruct him to say, 'I'm not interested,' and just leave.". . .

Can new laws successfully address the problem? The Exon amendment is very broad. It could hamper communication between adults—the essence of online activity—and might not even solve the problems that kids face. "It would be a mistake to drive us, in a moment of hysteria, to a solution that is unconstitutional, would stultify technology, and wouldn't even fulfill its mission," argues Jerry Berman, director of the Center for Democracy and Technology. . . .

High-Tech Solutions

Can high-tech solutions help? Ultimately, James Exon's greatest contribution to the protection of children may not be his legislation but the fear it has created in Silicon Valley and its virtual environs. Already parents can buy some sophisticated software to block children's access to questionable material. More is on the way; Microsoft, Netscape and the Progressive Networks joined together to develop new prophylactic devices. "The Exon amendment certainly raised consciousness," says Mike Homer of Netscape. "But we believe there is a variety of fairly straightforward tools that would allow us to self-regulate." More than 100 companies have called, asking to help. Another, perhaps complementary, scheme in the works is KidCode, a means by which the addresses on the World Wide Web will have voluntary ratings embedded. "Places that provide erotica on the Internet are wild about the idea of voluntary ratings," says Nathaniel Borenstein, designer of KidCode. "They don't *want* to sell to kids."

Meanwhile, one solution has already hit the market: Surf-Watch, created by an eponymous Silicon Valley firm. Its software works by matching a potential Net destination to a proprietary list of forbidden sites. In addition, the $50 software package looks for objectionable language. Once parents or educators install it, they have at least one line of defense. "This is the kind of software that can offer the individual choice as opposed to censorship," says SurfWatch vice president Jay Friedland. . . .

Will the problem ever go away? The bottom line when it comes to kids, sex and the Internet is that no matter what laws we pass and what high-tech solutions we devise, the three of them together will never be less volatile than the first two alone. We can mitigate but not eliminate the drawbacks of high tech: there's no way to get its benefits without them.

It's a trade-off that Patricia Shao understands. In 1995, her 13-year-old daughter, visiting a friend, was in an online-service chat room when they were propositioned to have "cybersex." Shao was shocked, and even more so when her daughter casually told her, "This is what happens when we're online." "They thought it was just a crackpot," says Shao, a Bethesda, Md., marketing executive. Instead of pulling the cyberplug, however, Shao took pains to educate herself about online sex. She even engaged in some political activism, signing on with a pro-Exon anti-pornography group. And ultimately, Shao's family purchased its own America Online subscription *after* her daughter's close encounter with a pixilated stranger.

If there were more built-in programs like SurfWatch available to her, Shao says, she'd probably use them. But in the meantime she is making do with the more old-fashioned method of talking to her kids—and trusting them. "I've warned my children about the obscene material out there, and I trust them not to access it." As careful parents will do, she monitors the family online activity somewhat, by tracking the hours they are logged on. But as with other passages—going out alone, driving a car—ultimately, you have to let kids grow up. Even if some of the growing up happens online.

---

*"Opponents of computer pornography laws say
we should simply 'empower' parents. . . . This is
a bad idea."*

Parents Should Not Have to Protect Children from Internet Pornography

Cathleen A. Cleaver

Cathleen A. Cleaver is the director of legal studies at the Family Research Council, a national organization that promotes traditional, conservative family values through lobbying and public education efforts. Cleaver, an attorney, litigated child pornography cases with her former employer, the National Law Center for Children and Families. In the following viewpoint, Cleaver states that Internet pornography poses many threats to society. Parents alone cannot carry the burden of protecting children from computer pornography, she argues. Cleaver concludes that laws must be passed to rid the Internet of pornography.

As you read, consider the following questions:

1. How does Cleaver refute the belief that censorship of pornography could lead to censorship of art?
2. Why does Cleaver oppose relying solely on parents to regulate Internet pornography?
3. How does the author respond to the argument that laws censoring Internet pornography will not work?

From Cathleen A. Cleaver, "FBI Child Porn Stings and a Virtual Denial of Reality," *Perspective*, September 14, 1995. Reprinted by permission of the author and the Family Research Council.

With a few clicks of the mouse, today's computer novice can get raw, even violent, sexual images once difficult to find without exceptional effort and material risk. The user can go to popular "erotica" sites to fill his screens with photographs of group sex scenes, close-up shots of genital mutilation, eroticized defecation scenarios, or vulgar videotape stills of animals with young women. He can sell these pictures, or swap them, or send them to disturb a neighbor, or post them to shock the unwary. The user can meet inquisitive children in chat rooms and send them lewd photographs of himself. He can write detailed accounts of rape and murder and display them for all to read. The user can do these things in near anonymity, and with the comfort of knowing that he is not at risk of legal sanction. This is cyberspace now, and it is the free speech absolutist's dreamworld.

Most concede that obscenity—hard-core sexual material so graphic and unredeeming that it fails the Supreme Court's test—should be illegal on computers as it is elsewhere. Others balk, however, at the proposition of laws to keep computer indecency from children. It is a feigned reaction. "Indecency" is legal for adults, but can be regulated so that it is kept from children. It has been defined as *a pattern of patently offensive depictions or descriptions of sexual or excretory activities or organs.* The hysterical arguments about indecency laws banning serious works of literature or library art are no more credible now than they were when unsuccessfully lobbed at such laws in other contexts. Society has long embraced the principle that those who peddle harmful material have the obligation to keep the material from children. Moreover, to charge, as some do, that indecency regulation will bring the developing technology to a screeching halt is to maintain that its advancement *depends upon* unfettered exhibition of offensive sexual material. This cannot be true.

Empowering Parents: A Bad Idea

Opponents of computer pornography laws say we should simply "empower" parents instead. They would empower parents by forcing them to purchase expensive software products to try to combat the pornographers themselves. This is a bad idea for several reasons. It is bad philosophically because it advocates *restricting* the behavior of the "good guys" (families and children) while giving license to the "bad guys" to litter cyberspace with pornography. It also represents a drastic departure from time-honored principles of the role of law in protecting children from exploitation. Outside cyberspace, laws restrain people from displaying sexually explicit images in public places and from selling alcohol, tobacco, or porn magazines to children. No one suggests that parents are absolved from parental responsibility because of these laws. Yet, in the cyberporn debate, a small cho-

123

rus of angry voices bellows: "It's the responsibility of *parents,* not government!" when identical laws are considered.

It is also a bad idea to leave the burden completely on the parent, because it will not work. Without liability and penalty disincentives, the ability to restrict pornography would depend upon the character of pornography distributors. Already there are electronic "how-to" pamphlets to circumvent blocking devices. As technical restrictions increase, so too will these aids, and they will be marketed and used with impunity.

Reprinted by permission of Mike Ramirez and Copley News Service.

We can observe first-hand what the result of a purely market-based, non-regulatory solution would look like, for we are looking at it now. Those advocating technofixes in place of laws aren't earnestly seeking to empower parents to protect children. Rather, they want to force parents by the power of their arrogance to kick kids off of this universal system so that nothing need inhibit the free porn trade.

The Superhighway Is Not for Pornographers

Opponents of pornography laws implore that the laws simply cannot apply to this new medium. This tattered old argument is pulled out and dusted off with each new technological advance. We saw it last in the early '80s with the advent of the commercial videotape market, and we see it now again. Scientific change mandates legal change only insofar as it affects the justification for a law. The notion that people who disseminate harmful material have the obligation to restrict the material from children is one which transcends specific technology. Old laws might need definition and renovation, but old principles stand firm.

Cyberspace is a work in progress. We should not squander the opportunity to examine and appreciate a world where pornography knows no bounds. The information superhighway does not belong to pornographers. Failure to enact strong laws is a concession that it should.

"Enforcing laws against obscenity . . . will help ensure that the information superhighway will enhance our lives."

Strong Laws Are Needed to Control Internet Pornography

Robert W. Peters

Robert W. Peters is the president of Morality in Media, Inc., a national interfaith organization that works to curb traffic in illegal hard-core pornography and to uphold standards of decency in the media. In the following viewpoint, Peters argues that pornography on the Internet harms society and should be regulated through strong obscenity laws. Peters concludes that most Americans do not want to see sexual violence on the Internet and would welcome any measures to control such pornography.

As you read, consider the following questions:

1. How does Peters both criticize and praise the television of the 1950s and 1960s?
2. What does Morality in Media propose as a way to control pornography on the information superhighway, according to the author?
3. How did the U.S. Supreme Court distinguish between protected works and unprotected pornography in its *Miller v. California* decision, as cited by Peters?

From Robert W. Peters, "Information Superhighway or Technological Sewer: What Will It Be?" *Federal Communications Law Journal*, vol. 47, no. 2, December 1994. Reprinted with permission.

Several years ago the host of a radio talk show asked me whether I was an expert "on the media" or just on the subject of indecency in the media. I responded without hesitation that my expertise was the latter. In recent years, I have become interested in a broader range of media issues, but my focus—and that of Morality in Media—is still very much the subject of indecency in the media. It is also, in good measure, the focus of this viewpoint.

I was brought up in the 1950s and 1960s, during what some refer to as television's golden years, and our family certainly watched a lot of television. Thinking back, however, I can't remember much, if anything, other than perhaps too much violence, that I saw on TV that I would now consider morally objectionable.

Glorification and promotion of sexual immorality, vulgarity, nudity, and sexually explicit scenes just weren't part of the programming, as I remember it. The television industry, for whatever reasons, had high regard for standards of decency and, generally speaking, for the Judeo-Christian moral and family ethic.

Not Real Life

I agree with those who say that real life for many if not most Americans in the 1950s and 1960s had little to do with "life" on primetime TV. The real-life problems were often bigger and not so easily solved, and most real-life American families weren't so well-off financially. Nor did all live in "lily-white" suburbs.

But the "domestic environment" presented on television in the 1950s and 1960s was, on the whole, constructive, well-mannered, and likeable, and television was a source of entertainment that the vast majority of Americans could enjoy, with or without their children, and that did not offend their most cherished values.

Today, opinion polls show that Americans are no longer comfortable with much TV programming. For example, according to a Family Channel/Gallup Survey released in July 1993, an almost two-to-one majority of viewers said that TV depicts negative values over positive ones, and an even larger percentage felt that TV programming does not represent their own values. According to a survey from the Corporation for Public Broadcasting, released in January 1994, 82 percent of adults think TV is too violent and 70 percent think there is too much sex and offensive language.

More recently, a June 1994 *Newsweek* poll reported that in response to the question "Who is to blame for the problem of low morals and personal character in this country?" 67 percent "blame" TV and other popular entertainment "a lot." Both the President and First Lady have expressed their concern about the level of violence and explicit sex on TV, which should help dispel any notion that the concern is limited to constituents of the "religious right."

Not What the Public Wants

This and other evidence of widespread concern about exploitive, gratuitous sex, vulgarity, and violence on TV and in other media should also put to rest the notion that the entertainment media are giving the American people what they want. As a dear friend once put it: "It is preposterous to suggest that TV viewers are bombarding the TV producers with demands for more sexual dysfunctionals on talk shows, or more graphic depictions of sex and violence in TV movies, or more four-letter words in sitcoms and dramas." A 1992 Gallup Poll showed that 71 percent of Americans say that objectionable content influences them to watch less TV.

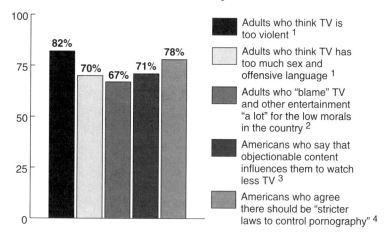

Public Views on Morality and the Media

- Adults who think TV is too violent [1]
- Adults who think TV has too much sex and offensive language [1]
- Adults who "blame" TV and other entertainment "a lot" for the low morals in the country [2]
- Americans who say that objectionable content influences them to watch less TV [3]
- Americans who agree there should be "stricter laws to control pornography" [4]

Sources: 1. January 1994 survey by the Corporation for Public Broadcasting; 2. June 1994 *Newsweek* poll; 3. 1992 Gallup poll; 4. June 1994 *Wall Street Journal*/NBC News poll.

I would add that it is a mistake to assume that because viewers regularly watch a program, they must enjoy or approve of all of it. For example, I still very much enjoy a good football game. I don't, however, enjoy watching players get knocked unconscious or seriously injured, and if the sport continues to get more and more violent, I will stop watching it.

I point out the above because the moguls of the communications industry must make policymaking decisions, not just in regard to technology, but also in regard to program content. The financially profitable, as well as socially responsible, decision would be to provide more and more uplifting, wholesome entertainment—not more and more indecent, violent fare. . . .

It is our earnest desire that the leaders of the mainstream communications industry will once again make decisions about program content, not on the basis of what is profitable in the short run, but on the basis of what is profitable *and* socially beneficial—or, at the very least, not socially destructive.

Unfortunately, however, not everyone has a social conscience. That is why we have laws, and at Morality in Media, we don't agree that the information superhighway should be exempt from laws prohibiting obscenity or indecency. There are already laws prohibiting or restricting obscene or indecent matter in the broadcast media, on cable/satellite TV, and by means of telephone. To the extent that new technologies have created "loopholes," laws should be enacted to plug them. For example, the current federal obscenity laws may be inadequate to address the growing problem of noncommercial computer "bulletin boards" that provide hardcore pornographic material. We have prepared a proposed law to address this problem.

At Morality in Media, we also don't agree that the obscenity laws should only be enforced against sleazy "adults only" businesses, but not against "mainstream" businesses that choose to profit from hardcore pornography—which includes so-called "cable versions" of hardcore material. According to a June 1994 WSJ/NBC News Poll, 78 percent of the American people agree that there should be "stricter laws to control pornography," and a major part of the concern can be directly tied to the decision of mainstream companies to promote and/or serve as distribution channels for hardcore pornography.

The Intrusiveness of Obscenity

We also read *FCC v. Pacifica Foundation* as allowing the government to prohibit non-obscene but "indecent" material on the information superhighway in circumstances where unwilling adults would be assaulted in the privacy of their home and/or children would have easy access to it. The rationale for our position was aptly described by our current General Counsel, Paul J. McGeady:

> Does not the Supreme Court opinion [in *Miller v. California*] mean that you can present explicit hard-core sex . . . on TV if the "play" or "film" or "live performance" [when taken as a whole] has literary or artistic value? It would appear that most Americans . . . would not tolerate the concept that they must switch the dial to avoid such performances on TV or radio or that they must be concerned that their minor children may be exposed. . . . Television and radio communications . . . partake

of the nature of a public access thoroughfare (albeit an electro-magnetic one), and what may be prohibited on the public street should be equally prohibited on TV and radio. This includes undoubtedly all soft-core or hard-core sexually explicit conduct as well as nudity. . . . What is the quality in public nudity that permits the law to inhibit it without proof of obscenity? . . . We suggest that the quality involved is "Intrusiveness.". . . Just as a citizen is entitled to walk down the public street without the necessity of having to avert his eyes to avoid a public nude performance, so too he [or she] is entitled to "flip the dial" without viewing intrusive nudity or explicit hard-core sex.

Enforcing laws against obscene or indecent material over the information superhighway will not prevent the discussion of human sexuality or the presentation of any viewpoint pertaining thereto. As the Supreme Court pointed out in *FCC v. Pacifica Foundation*, "[a] requirement that indecent language be avoided will have its primary effect on the form, rather than the content, of serious communication."

Preventing the Creation of a High-Tech Sewer

The time of day and other factors are also important in determining whether a particular depiction or description is "indecent." Under the holding of *Sable Communications v. FCC*, indecent but non-obscene communications by means of telephone are protected in circumstances where they are restricted to adults who seek them.

As for the "communicative content" of obscene expression, the Supreme Court in its *Miller v. California* decision stated aptly:

The First Amendment protects works which, taken as a whole, have serious literary, artistic, political or scientific value, regardless of whether the government or the majority of the people approve of the ideas these works represent. "The protection given speech and press was fashioned to assure unfettered interchange of ideas for the bringing about of political and social changes desired by the people," [the court stated in *Roth v. United States*]. . . . But the public portrayal of hard-core sexual conduct for its own sake, and for the ensuing commercial gain, is a different matter.

Enforcing laws against obscenity or indecency, however, will help ensure that the information superhighway will enhance our lives, rather than transforming our cultural environment into a toxic, technological sewer—or, perhaps more accurately, a public nuisance. Law enforcement will help discourage the "permissiveness" which, as Chief Justice Warren Burger stated, can only "tend further to erode public confidence in the law—that subtle but indispensable ingredient of ordered liberty."

"Make it a regulator's job . . . to surf the Net looking out for material that would be prohibited if supplied in traditional ways."

Strong Laws Are Not Needed to Control Internet Pornography

The Economist

In the following viewpoint, the editors of the *Economist* agree that pornography on the Internet must be regulated. They disagree, however, that strong anti-pornography laws are the solution. Instead, the editors argue, regulators could be appointed to find Internet pornography and to inform providers of its existence. These providers could then limit consumers' access to such materials. The *Economist* is a British weekly magazine of economic and political analysis and opinion.

As you read, consider the following questions:

1. What is the danger of heavy-handed anti-pornography legislation, in the *Economist*'s opinion?
2. What problems do the authors see in allowing users to self-control their access to Internet pornography?
3. What flaws do the authors see in their own proposal?

Censorship is an ugly word. But even liberal societies accept the need for governments to uphold some standards of public decency and, in particular, to shield children from exposure to the worst obscenities. Almost everywhere, governments restrict what can be pumped out on radio, film and television, or down the telephone line, or in books and periodicals. Should cyberspace be any different?

There is no obvious reason to exempt the Internet and other computer networks from restrictions that society chooses to clamp on other forms of communication. But neither is there reason to treat cyberspace less liberally than other media—by means, for instance, of the bill that sailed through America's Senate and would, if it became law, threaten people who send "indecent" words or pictures via computers with a fine of $100,000 and up to two years in prison. [This bill was amended and became part of the 1996 Telecommunications Reform Act.] This is clumsy and heavy-handed. Such a law could kill the chances of the Internet developing into a superb vehicle for free speech and open communications.

The alternative proposed by many supporters of the Internet is self-control. They put their faith in software programs that block access to pornographic "sites" on the Internet, or in senders voluntarily labelling Internet material that is not appropriate for children. Some commercial services, such as America Online, already allow parents to make some "adult" areas off-limits to children. These private (as opposed to official) remedies are welcome, though it remains to be seen how well they will work. The trouble is that all of them place the technical burden of screening cyberspace's offerings on users (lists of "indecent" sites would require constant updating), and they take no account of regional differences in the definition of obscenity (stuff that is deemed obscene in America might be considered tame in Denmark, risqué in Britain and outrageous in Saudi Arabia).

The Difference Between Cannot and Should Not

Why then not regulate the Net like other media? Nerds, who revere the anarchic character of the Net, think any interference whatever is wrong. More telling, they claim (convenient, this) that the Internet cannot be policed even if it should be.

Certainly, the Net is more difficult to regulate than traditional media. It is unfettered by national boundaries. More important, once connected to it, all you need to become a large-scale supplier of pornography is a personal computer. Governments can control the output of TV stations by withholding licences; they can raid presses or close cinemas. Policing the millions of computer-owners who might want to post something nasty in cyberspace does indeed seem impossible.

Nonetheless, the view that nothing can be done is probably wrong—and, for the Internet's own sake, it had better be. If current proposals are any guide, rules of an extremely illiberal sort are a likelier outcome in many countries than the present free-for-all, if that remains the only choice. So here is a better idea. It concentrates on the role of Internet "access providers", the firms that make their living by hooking local subscribers on to the Net. Some current proposals aim to make these providers liable for infringements they cannot prevent: even if it were desirable (which it isn't), providers could not monitor millions of files each day, screening out everything that might be deemed objectionable. But there is another approach.

Reprinted by permission of the artist.

Make it a regulator's job, guided by users' complaints, to surf the Net looking out for material that would be prohibited if supplied in traditional ways. When such material is discovered, access providers could be alerted, and required to deny users entry to the sites concerned. Safeguards would be needed: the regulator's actions would have to be overseen by a court, with opportunities for legal challenge. Other protections could be built in.

The limits of any such scheme are clear. First, regulators could control only those providers that fall within their national jurisdiction. At the greater expense of an international (as opposed to local) telephone call, a porn-seeker could find an unregulated provider based abroad. A determined censor would then need to block access to those foreign providers—a large and worrying extension of his powers. As the cost of telecommunications continues to fall, this loophole will grow, and the dilemma for those wishing to balance desirable regulation against broader freedoms will be more painful.

The scheme is flawed in other respects too. Some parts of public cyberspace (notably live chat areas and broadcast e-mail) may be impossible to regulate even in this limited way. And no matter how great its appetite for obscenity, no regulator could hope to find all, or even most, offending sites. However, to judge the idea by these standards would be silly. Existing regimes of media regulation are themselves extremely imperfect. When they make sense, it is certainly not because they prevent all contact with prohibited material. It is because they make obscenity more difficult to find, especially by accident; and because this greater difficulty (especially where children are concerned) serves a social purpose. With a little ingenuity, a similar result can be achieved in cyberspace.

Periodical Bibliography

The following articles have been selected to supplement the diverse views presented in this chapter. Addresses are provided for periodicals not indexed in the *Readers' Guide to Periodical Literature*, the *Alternative Press Index*, or the *Social Sciences Index*.

Edmund L. Andrews	"A Crusader Against Cyberporn Who Was Once Involved in a Sex Scandal," *New York Times*, November 27, 1995.
Joe Chidley	"Red-Light District," *Maclean's*, May 22, 1995.
Thomas J. DeLoughry	"Existing Laws Called Adequate to Bar Children's Access to On-Line Pornography," *Chronicle of Higher Education*, August 4, 1995. Available from 1255 23rd St. NW, Suite 700, Washington, DC 20037.
Edwin Diamond	"Law and Order Comes to Cyberspace," *Technology Review*, October 1995.
Philip Elmer-DeWitt	"On a Screen Near You: Cyberporn—It's Popular, Pervasive, and Surprisingly Perverse," *Time*, July 3, 1995.
Amy Harmon	"The 'Seedy' Side of CD-ROMs," *Los Angeles Times*, November 29, 1993. Available from Reprints, Times Mirror Square, Los Angeles, CA 90053.
Stephen Labaton	"As Pornography Arrests Grow, So Do Plans for Computer Stings," *New York Times*, September 16, 1995.
Steve Lohr	"The Net: It's Hard to Clean Up," *New York Times*, June 18, 1995.
Michael Meyer	"A Bad Dream Comes True in Cyberspace," *Newsweek*, January 8, 1996.
Joshua Quittner	"How Parents Can Filter Out the Naughty Bits," *Time*, July 3, 1995.
Joshua Quittner	"Vice Raid on the Net," *Time*, April 3, 1995.
Frank Rich	"Newt to the Rescue," *New York Times*, July 1, 1995.
Jared Sandberg	"FBI Crackdown on Computer Child Pornography Opens Hornet's Nest, Stinging America Online," *Wall Street Journal*, September 15, 1995.
Washington Watch	"Smut: Out-of-Line Online," February 26, 1996. Available from the Family Research Council, 700 13th St. NW, Suite 500, Washington, DC 20005.

What Should Be the Feminist Stance on Pornography?

Pornography

Chapter Preface

Feminists have long worked to gain sexual freedom for women. In the early 1900s, Margaret Sanger strove to increase the availability and acceptance of birth control. In the 1960s and early 1970s, the women's movement endeavored to help women learn about and express their sexuality.

The issue of pornography was largely ignored during these years. Then, in the late 1970s, some feminists, led by Andrea Dworkin and Catharine MacKinnon, began pointing to pornography as a cause of sexual harassment and violence against women. These anti-pornography feminists believed, in Dworkin's words, that "pornography is the graphic, sexually explicit subordination of women that includes a series of scenarios, . . . from women being dehumanized—turned into objects and commodities—through women showing pleasure in being raped, through the dismemberment of women." Today anti-pornography feminists continue to advocate banning or strictly regulating pornography—especially hard-core and violent pornography.

Other feminists have refused to join the anti-pornography movement. These feminists argue that censoring pornography contradicts feminism's goals by repressing rather than liberating sexual expression. Nadine Strossen, president of the American Civil Liberties Union and the author of the book *Defending Pornography*, believes that the anti-pornography feminists hold "a very fearful, very negative view of human sexuality, especially female sexuality. What troubles me is their fundamental view of human nature, which is a very authoritarian one. They believe that we all are irresponsible, incapable of making the right choice, and so they have taken it upon themselves to make those decisions for us." Strossen and other feminists argue that fighting censorship, not pornography, will further women's rights.

The crux of the debate among feminists is whether women need to be protected from pornography or whether they benefit from the sexual freedom it may represent. The contributors in the following chapter address this issue. The views of Dworkin and MacKinnon are not included in this chapter because they believe pornography indisputably oppresses women. Consequently, in their opinion, the question addressed here is not a matter of debate.

"Interviews [conducted with men about their pornography use] illuminate and provide support for the feminist anti-pornography critique."

Feminists Should Oppose Pornography

Robert Jensen

Robert Jensen is an assistant professor in the journalism department at the University of Texas at Austin. He is a coeditor of the book *Freeing the First Amendment: Critical Perspectives on Freedom of Expression*. In the following viewpoint, Jensen presents his findings from interviews with sex offenders and with men who use pornography. Jensen believes that the interviews provide strong anecdotal evidence that pornography can lead to sexually aberrant behavior and sexually violent crimes. He concludes that the anti-pornography stance taken by some feminists is correct.

As you read, consider the following questions:

1. On what grounds does Jensen criticize laboratory studies of the effects of pornography on behavior?
2. How does Craig, one of the men interviewed by the author, describe what his view of women was prior to his arrest?
3. In what specific ways can the use of pornography be linked to sexual violence, according to Jensen?

I went to a porno bookstore, put a quarter in a slot, and saw this porn movie. It was just a guy coming up from behind a girl and attacking her and raping her. That's when I started having rape fantasies. When I seen that movie, it was like somebody lit a fuse from my childhood on up. When that fuse got to the porn movie, I exploded. I just went for it, went out and raped. It was like a little voice saying, "It's all right, it's all right, go ahead and rape and get your revenge; you'll never get caught. Go out and rip off some girls. It's all right; they even make movies of it."

—from T. Beneke, *Men on Rape*, 1982

In the contemporary debate over pornography and its effects, words like those of "Chuck," a 28-year-old convicted rapist, often are dismissed as merely anecdotal and of limited value in understanding sexually explicit material. This viewpoint argues that narrative accounts are one of our best sources of information about the connection between pornography and violence against women. It reports on 24 interviews conducted with men about their pornography use. When analyzed in conjunction with narrative accounts of women's experiences with pornography, these interviews illuminate and provide support for the feminist anti-pornography critique. The narratives discussed in this viewpoint give specific examples of how pornography can (a) be an important factor in shaping a male-dominant view of sexuality, (b) contribute to a user's difficulty in separating sexual fantasy and reality, (c) be used to initiate victims and break down their resistance to sexual activity, and (d) provide a training manual for abusers.

The Feminist Critique of Pornography

After decades of unproductive sparring between liberals and conservatives, all framed by the moral and legal concept of obscenity, a feminist critique of pornography based on a radical approach to sexuality emerged during the late 1970s and 1980s. Highlighting how pornography sexualizes male dominance and female submission, this critique sees pornography as a kind of sexist hate literature, the expression of a male sexuality rooted in the subordination of women, that endorses the sexual objectification of, and can promote sexual violence against, women. Controversy about this approach focused on an anti-pornography ordinance, written by Andrea Dworkin and Catharine MacKinnon, that identified pornography as "a practice of sex discrimination" and a "systematic practice of exploitation and subordination based on sex that differentially harms and disadvantages women." The ordinance met with varied success in several cities but has been rejected by the federal courts.

One of the most important aspects of the political organizing around the ordinance was the creation of a public space for women to talk about how pornography had affected their lives. In Minneapolis, Minnesota, the first city to consider the ordinance, those women spoke in hearings before a city council committee. Instead of relying solely on experimental research on the connection between pornography and sexual violence, the anti-pornography organizers asked that attention be paid to the lived experience of women who had been victimized.

The present research is rooted in that radical feminist approach to pornography and sexuality. I argue that instead of privileging the experimental laboratory research that has been so prominent in the debate over pornography during the past three decades, we should look to richly detailed narrative accounts of women and men that can tell us a great deal about how pornography works in the world. Elsewhere, I have criticized such experimental work. Unlike many critics of these studies, who argue that any connection between pornography and sexual violence found in the lab is probably overstated, I suggest that we should be at least as concerned that lab studies underestimate pornography's role in promoting misogynistic attitudes and behavior.

First, these studies are incapable of measuring subtle effects that develop over time. If pornography's main effect is the shaping of attitudes and behavior after repeated exposure, there is no guarantee that studies exposing people to a small amount of pornography over a short time can accurately measure anything. Also, no lab can reproduce the natural setting of the behavior being studied. How is watching a pornographic movie in a university video lab (the experience of experimental subjects) different from viewing it in the living room of a fraternity house where a group of young men might watch a pornographic videotape while drinking beer and urging each other to enjoy the tape? And how does the act of masturbating to pornography, a common male experience, influence the way in which men interpret and are affected by pornography?

Research Is Not Impartial

If experimental data seem to suggest, for example, that exposure to depictions in which women appear to enjoy being raped can increase men's acceptance of sexual violence against women and increase men's endorsement of that rape myth, can we assume those effects will be even more pronounced on a man who views that same sexual material in a real-world environment in which male aggression is often encouraged and sanctioned? The problems are compounded if one acknowledges that research, no matter what its claims, can never be impartial and objective and always is value laden. Researchers generally accept a mainstream definition of what is to be considered "normal" sexuality.

Whereas the existence of sexual drive and interests is in some ways "natural" or biologically based, the form our sexual practices take is socially constructed, and that construction in this culture is rooted in the politics of gender. Relying on the majority view to determine what is erotic implicitly endorses the sexual status quo, which means accepting patriarchal definitions.

This point about values often is used by sexual libertarians, who contend that by labeling practices such as sadomasochism "deviant," research is biased. But the critique also has to come from a different angle; in patriarchal society, what has been considered normal sex generally has been what serves to enhance men's pleasure; the line between normal intercourse and deviant rape can be a fine one. Researchers must make value judgments about what is erotic, nonviolent, and normal, and those decisions define what is a deviant, unhealthy, callous, or socially undesirable response to the material. It is not that any specific researcher blunders by letting value judgments in but that such research always makes normative judgments about sexuality.

Pornography Is Implicated

It is important to be clear about what I suggest narratives can tell us. Such accounts do not prove, in a direct causal sense, that pornography causes sexual violence. They do, however, show how pornography is implicated in the abusive behavior of some men. This viewpoint does not contend that all sex abusers use pornography or that all pornography users will become sex abusers; proponents of the feminist anti-pornography critique have never made such simplistic assertions. But the narratives do suggest that for some sex abusers, pornography is an integral part of their abuse.

The full value of men's narratives is realized when they are combined with the women's accounts and when we all compare and contrast those accounts with our own experiences with pornography. This endeavor may not provide the "truth" about pornography, but as Lorraine Code suggests, "there may be no facts of the matter in any absolute sense, either in science or in law, and . . . it really all amounts to telling plausible stories." We can work toward knowing which stories are more plausible than others; rejecting truth need not involve rejecting the possibility of identifying true stories. Donald Polkinghorne echoes that approach when he acknowledges that an inquiry based in narrative accounts should not claim to have uncovered a single objective account of reality: "The argument does not produce certainty; it produces likelihood."

This project included two sets of interviews. In both cases, subjects were anonymous (except for those who volunteered their names; all names in this viewpoint are pseudonyms), and the interviews were tape recorded. The first 11 interviews (the "pornography users" group) were with men who responded to a classified ad in the personals section of the two Minneapolis–St. Paul entertainment weeklies. The ad asked for male interview subjects who "read or view any sexually explicit material." The second set of interviews (the "sex offenders" group) was with 13 residents of the Alpha Human Services sex offender treatment program in Minneapolis. . . . I focus on cases in which the links between pornography use and abuse were most clear. . . .

Craig

"Craig" was a 34-year-old heterosexual lumber worker who had never been married. He grew up in a small town in a rural area and went as far as the 10th grade in school. He was raised Catholic but no longer considered himself a religious person and had no interest in political issues. Craig had the most violent and abusive sexual history of the men with whom I talked. He had beaten and raped prostitutes, violently raped other women, used drugs and coercion to have sex with teenage girls, and sexually abused young girls.

Craig's first exposure to pornography came at age 7 or 8 when he found a box of *Playboy*, *Penthouse*, and *Hustler* magazines in a hayloft of an abandoned farm. From that point, he continually used those and other magazines that he shoplifted from stores. During his early teens, he began sneaking into an adult bookstore to watch videos. During his later teens, he continued to use magazines, sometimes masturbating to them in his parked car while he watched girls on the street.

Pornography and Violence

At age 18, Craig joined the marines and, at about the same time, began heavy consumption of explicit pornography including violent pornography. He compared the "rush" of violent pornography to similar feelings he experienced taking drugs. Shortly after that, he also began using prostitutes, sometimes paying a higher price to be allowed to tie up the women and whip them. He later repeated that behavior with women who were not prostitutes, beating them up "because towards the last [before his arrest], that was the only way I could get aroused." He said the pornography use and visits to prostitutes were roughly at the same time: "When I got into it heavy, the pornography and the prostitutes kind of fell in together. I believe the pornography came first."

From about age 21 on, Craig's pornography use centered on explicit videotapes he watched at home. He said he liked a variety of sexual acts on the screen but preferred that the men in the movies always be in control, fast-forwarding past scenes of women in control: "It was like it was a threat to me, to have a woman [in control]." He said that was also a factor in his use of bondage pornography: "The control you had, to put the women in any position you wanted, to force her to do anything."

Craig recently had been involved in a long-term relationship, but the woman left him because of his violent behavior. He said he thought some of his ideas for sexual activity, such as his constant desire for women to perform oral sex on him, were sparked at least in part by the pornography he used:

> There was a lot of oral sex that I wanted her to perform on me. There were, like, ways that would entice it in the movies, and I tried to use that on her, and it wouldn't work. Sometimes I'd get frustrated, and that's when I started hitting her. . . . I used a lot of force, a lot of direct demands, that in the movies women would just cooperate. And I would demand stuff from her. And if she didn't, I'd start slapping her around.

While in his 20s, Craig also began using child pornography obtained from underground sources. His sexual activity also began to focus more on children, usually girls in their early teens. Eventually, he abused girls as young as age 7. At some point, he began to use pornography and women or girls together: "Towards the end, it was so exhilarating to me to have the pornography and the child at the same time or the woman at the same time . . . and sometimes I have a longing for that feeling, the complete exhilaration, my whole body goes numb I'm so excited."

Made for Sex

Craig described his view of women before his arrest as "that they were made for sex, and that's all. I grew up with that attitude. . . . [My older brother] kept saying over and over that women are for sex. Use them and throw them away. I thrived on that."

Craig was reluctant to blame his behavior on pornography, but he emphasized its importance in shaping his sexuality as a child and its continuing influence on him as an adult:

> It's like it all stemmed from when I was growing up, watching the movies, pornography. . . . Once I saw the materials, it's like I got new ideas. It's like it reinforced my thinking. . . . But it was my choice to react to it. I don't think the pornography made me do what I did. I made the decision to do it. I could have talked to people and let them know what my thinking was, and I possibly could have got help a lot sooner. But I had to keep this a big secret. I could control this; I'm this super-being. . . .

Kevin

"Kevin" was a 24-year-old single heterosexual man who had most recently worked as a school bus driver. He had attended 1 year of college and 1 year of vocational-technical school after graduating from high school in the suburb where he grew up. He was raised Catholic but did not consider himself religious any longer, and he described himself as a conservative Republican. Kevin was convicted of the sexual abuse of two 6-year-old girls, and he said he had committed several other rapes and acts of sexual abuse.

Satisfying Men's Need for Revenge

My whole reason for being in the [pornography] Industry is to satisfy the desire of the men in the world who basically don't much care for women and want to see the men in my Industry getting even with the women they couldn't have when they were growing up. I strongly believe this, and the Industry hates me for saying it. . . . So we . . . somewhat brutalize a woman sexually: we're getting even for their [the male viewers'] lost dreams. I believe this. I've heard audiences cheer me when I do something foul on screen. When I've strangled a person or sodomized a person or brutalized a person, the audience is cheering my action, and then when I've fulfilled my warped desire, the audience applauds.

R. Stoller, *Porn: Myths for the Twentieth Century*, 1991.

Kevin had the most extensive and most constant use of pornography of the men interviewed. His first viewing of pornographic material was at age 11 when he and a friend found the friend's father's collection of *Playboy* magazines. From an ad in *Playboy*, he sent away to a mail-order company for 8-millimeter movies, using his name and his friend's address. Kevin said that when he ordered movies, he signed a form stating he was 18 years old. Because his friend's parents were divorced and the mother was often not home, they could use that address for orders and watch the movies there. By the time he was age 14 or 15, he looked old enough to buy magazines, including *Hustler*, in stores. During his high school years, he also began buying explicit videotapes, which he watched both alone and with groups of male friends.

Men Bossing Women

After high school, Kevin began buying sexually explicit magazines and patronizing the 25-cent movie booths at adult bookstores. During recent years, he also had begun calling phone sex lines. At the time of his arrest, he had 50 to 75 magazines, about a dozen videotapes, and a handful of 8-millimeter movies in his closet. He had looked at the magazines every day and had watched a movie at least twice a week. The movies consisted of explicit depictions of sex including group sex and ostensibly lesbian scenes. He described the interaction between men and women in these videotaped movies:

> The man would be the boss, and the woman would just do exactly what he said. And it was more of a subtle violence. . . . On the movies, it gives you the impression that if the woman hadn't agreed to what the man said, then he was capable of being very violent. There'd be some slapping and hair pulling and stuff. But not like the ones in 8-millimeter, where they really got some really violent things on there, like smack them over the head.

Kevin said the typical women were

> portrayed like they were just sex dolls, or whatever, just laying there on the bed. . . . The man would walk up and the woman would just kind of be brain-dead, do whatever the man said. Either they would just do it, and she would, like it was a reflex. Or he would boss her around, or whatever, and say, "You do this, you do that, bend over, roll over," whatever the case may be.

Violent Pornography

Kevin said he sometimes bought movies and magazines in discount packs without knowing anything about the content. Although he said he did not seek out violent pornography, he occasionally received such material in those packs and watched it. Those movies included scenes with women tied to beds, with men using whips and handcuffs on them and penetrating them with objects such as pop bottles—"stuff I thought was kind of sick in a way, at the time, but as I got more into it, I got more . . . into it." He described one of those movies:

> One that sticks out in my mind right now was really violent. There was pistol whipping and [a man] chained this woman up to a, had her in a doghouse, chained up like a dog in a doghouse, and this guy would come out and stick her head in the dog bowl and then have sex with her from behind. . . . At first I thought it was disgusting, but then as time wore on I did get into it more. I got excited by it more.

In his own sex life during his late teens and early 20s, Kevin relied on manipulative techniques with teenage girls; he traded drugs for sex on several different occasions with four or five girls ranging in age from 10 to 16. He also raped a junior high school girl who had passed out at a party. When he could afford it, he also used prostitutes at a local massage parlor. During this time, he also began looking at younger girls in his neighborhood and fantasizing about them.

Women as Objects

Kevin described pornography as his introduction to, and main source of information about, sex:

I think the main thing I got out of it was that sex was good. . . . I also got out of it that women were objects. Women or girls or any female was an object. As long as you got what you wanted, everything was O.K. . . . If I got what I wanted, that was fine. Whatever they did or whatever they felt was their own business. At the time, I didn't really care as long as I got what I wanted out of it, got my jollies out of it.

Kevin said that, at some point, the pornography had started to bore him, which was when he began his abusive behavior. He described the progression of his thinking:

When I was masturbating to these pornography things, I would think about certain girls I had seen on the bus or ones I had sold drugs to, and I would think as I was looking at these pictures in these books, what would it be like to have this girl or whoever doing this, what I'm thinking about. . . . Just masturbating to the thought wasn't getting it for me anymore. I actually had to be a part of it or actually had to do something about it. . . .

I think a lot of it had to do with just, the pictures are pictures. They're not real. And a fantasy is a wish for reality. You're wishing this would be real. And I got to the point where I wanted it, I was so ingrained, I wanted it to be real, that I would start to associate what I was seeing on the picture with someone I knew or had seen or associated with. And then I think it turned from that, I would start to actually really think about, you know, like with the girls I committed the crime with, or other ones I'd see on the bus. Like sometimes after I'd see like a certain load of kids would get off the bus, I'd pick out a couple and I'd watch them or stop and look at the mirror and stare at them and stuff like that. I would think, later on in the day, I'd masturbate to some pornography, I'd just use that picture kind of as a mental, it's kind of a scenery or whatever, and I'd put in my mind, I'd put myself and whoever at the time I was thinking about, in that picture. . . .

And sometimes, even with the pornography and the young girls I wouldn't be satisfied and I'd go over to the prostitution place and get a woman, and I'd pay her and she'd do whatever I wanted and I wouldn't get in trouble or wouldn't get caught or she wouldn't say no, or whatever. I could just do whatever I wanted, I could do.

Kevin said he may have become a sex abuser even without his heavy use of pornography but that the pornography was "the straw that broke the camel's back.". . .

Pornography Shapes Views of Sexuality

The purpose of these narratives is not to suggest that a 1- or 2-hour interview can identify the causes of a person's history of sexual violence. My goal is not to focus on the individual and attempt a psychological profile that explains fully their actions.

Many of the men experienced abuse as children, which played a role in their own abusing, and countless other factors—including the culture's institutionalized misogyny—may have been crucial in leading them to abuse.

However, these interviews can help us identify ways in which pornography is an important factor in the construction of sexuality and gender relations—what men come to see as acceptable, exciting, or necessary sex. Pornography is not the only force in our society constructing sex and gender in these ways, but the use of it is a common experience in the lives of the men interviewed. These interviews identified specific ways in which the use of pornography can be linked to sexual violence. For these men, pornography was an important factor in shaping a male-dominant view of sexuality, and in several cases the material contributed to the men's difficulty in separating fantasy from reality. Pornography also was used by at least one of the men to initiate a victim and break down that young girl's resistance to sexual activity. For several others, it was used as a training manual for abuse, as sexual acts and ideas from pornography were incorporated into their sex lives.

Elsewhere, I have argued that it is politically diversionary and ultimately unproductive to expect that experimental social science research will tell us the truth about the connection between pornography and sexual violence. We would be better served by continuing to look to narrative accounts for help in understanding not only how sexually explicit media but how the whole range of images and representations in our society help shape sexual behavior. This project is a step toward that goal, meant to be read not in isolation from, but together with, narrative accounts of women and to be compared with the reader's own experiences. Such narratives also must be considered in light of analyses of pornographic texts and information available about the production of pornography, although because of the nature of the business, little work has been done on production.

This viewpoint has taken the view that study of those elements—production, content, and effects—supports the feminist anti-pornography critique.

"It is time for feminists . . . to abandon anti-pornography feminism."

Feminists Should Not Oppose Pornography

Lynne Segal

In the following viewpoint, Lynne Segal argues that feminists who oppose pornography are misguided. She insists that there is no evidence that pornography causes sexual violence against women and that censoring pornography discourages women from completely understanding and expressing their sexuality. By focusing on pornography as the source of problems for women, according to Segal, anti-pornography feminists downplay the more significant causes of women's subordination: the sexism and misogyny that pervade Western society. Segal has written numerous articles and books on feminism, including *Is the Future Female? Troubled Thoughts on Contemporary Feminism* and *Slow Motion: Changing Masculinities, Changing Men.* She is coeditor of the book *Sex Exposed: Sexuality and the Pornography Debate.*

As you read, consider the following questions:

1. How did the anti-pornography feminists redefine pornography, in Segal's opinion?
2. How will a blanket condemnation of pornography affect women sexually, according to Segal?
3. How does the anti-pornography stance help sexual offenders evade responsibility for their crimes, in the author's opinion?

From Lynne Segal, "False Promises: Anti-Pornography Feminism," *Socialist Register*, 1993. Reprinted by permission.

Few political movements sprung into life with more confidence and optimism than the Western women's liberation movements of the late 1960s and early 1970s. "Sisterhood," as Sheila Rowbotham enthusiastically declared back in 1973, "demands a new woman, a new culture, and a new way of living." Men, perhaps reluctantly, would be swept along as well, she continued: "We must not be discouraged by them. We must go our own way but remember we are going to have to take them with us. They learn slowly. They are like creatures who have just crawled out of their shells after millennia of protection. They are sore, tender and afraid." But today many people, women and men alike, are urging all of us to crawl right back into our shells—it's safer, we are told, to stay put, to seek protection, because there is no change in men's eternal and ubiquitous oppression of women. "Our status as a group relative to men has almost never, if ever, been changed from what it is," Catharine MacKinnon tells us, in 1992. After all these years, what has feminism achieved? Nothing.

The End of Optimism

Yet women's liberation unquestionably did expand everybody's horizons, forcing a redefinition of what is personal and what is political. And of course most things have changed for women, much of it due to the persistent pressure of organized feminism. As I argued in *Is the Future Female?*, however uneven and complicated the general achievement of feminist goals seeking women's autonomy and equality with men, they are now widely supported and respectable. A mere 20 years ago women lacked even the words to speak in our own interests, and attempts to do so invariably met with ridicule. Campaigns against sexual harassment and violence against women, for childcare provision, abortion rights and women's equality generally are all now familiar on trade union council agendas, however much recession and cutbacks in welfare have further entrenched working-class and ethnic minority women in increasing impoverishment. Women today are more aware of their rights, less ready to be exploited, and more aggressive.

Despite its own success, however, despair is the theme of much contemporary feminist writing. Once optimism starts to wane, former ways of seeing can quickly become obscured, even disappear altogether. Victories are no longer visible. With confidence in decline, new theoretical frameworks start replacing the old, frameworks which transform memory itself, the stories we tell of our own past, our ideas for the future. We have seen it happen in one radical movement after another since the close of the 1970s. Within feminism, nowhere is this more apparent than in the area of sexual politics. . . .

To the bewilderment of many of second-wave feminism's founding members (who were often ridiculed for their concern with their own orgasms in seeking to liberate "the suppressed power of female sexuality" from centuries of male-centered discourses and practices), pornography seemed to become the feminist issue of the 1980s. The critique of the sexism and the exploitation of women in the media made by women's liberation in the 1970s had indeed always been loud and prominent. After picketing the Miss World beauty contest as the decade kicked off, pin-ups, pornography, advertising, textbooks and religious beliefs and imagery, all—with spray gun and paint—were declared "offensive to women." In the 1970s feminists had not, however, sought legal restrictions on pornography, nor seen it as in any way uniquely symbolic of male dominance—the virgin bride, the happy housewife, the sexy secretary were all equally abhorrent. With the state and judiciary so comprehensively controlled by men, obscenity laws were known in any case to have always served to suppress the work, if not jail the organizers, of those fighting for women's own control of their fertility and sexuality. Objecting to all forms of sexist representations, feminists then set out to subvert a whole cultural landscape which, whether selling carpet sweepers, collecting census information or uncovering women's crotches, placed women as the subordinate sex.

Right-Wing Support

Pro-censorship feminists are supported—in their rhetoric and in their campaigns—by the same right-wing groups which attack art as 'pornographic' if it is not heterosexual and in every other way 'decent' and 'moral' (attacks never opposed by pro-censorship feminists). These groups assail today, as they have in the past, every effort to change or ameliorate the conditions of women's lives. . . . The neo-Puritan feminists profess a different agenda, yet welcome these allies. Together, they want to tell us what ideas, fantasies, words and images are right, for them and for each one of us.

Leanne Katz, *Crossroads*, March 1993.

Representatively, Ruth Wallsgrove, writing for *Spare Rib*, declared in 1977: "I believe we should not agitate for more laws against pornography, but should rather stand up together and say what we feel about it, and what we feel about our own sexuality, and force men to reexamine their own attitudes to sex and women implicit in their consumption of porn." This type of feminist emphasis on women's need to assert their own sexual needs and desires, however, and force men to discuss theirs, came to be overshadowed by, and entangled with, feminist concern with the issue of male violence by the close of the seventies. As I have described elsewhere, it was the popular writing of Robin Morgan and Susan Brownmiller in the USA in the mid-1970s which first made a definitive connection between pornography and male violence. It was in their writing that men's sexuality was made synonymous with male violence, and male violence was presented as, in itself, the key to male dominance. With pornography portrayed as the symbolic proof of the connection between male sexuality and male violence, anti-pornography campaigning was soon to become emblematic of this strand of feminism. It redefined "pornography" as material which depicts violence against women, and which is, in itself, violence against women.

Andrea Dworkin's *Pornography: Men Possessing Women* is still the single most influential text proclaiming this particular feminist view of pornography, in which "pornography" not only lies behind all forms of female oppression, but behind exploitation, murder and brutality throughout human history. Following through such logic to draft model feminist anti-pornography legislation—the Minneapolis Ordinance—Andrea Dworkin and Catharine MacKinnon define pornography as "the graphic sexually explicit subordination of women through pictures or words." Armed with this definition, they propose that any individual should be able to use the courts to seek financial redress against the producers or distributors of sexually explicit material if they can show it has caused them "harm."

Exploitation Preceded Pornography

And yet, despite the growth and strength of the feminist anti-pornography movement during the 1980s, particularly in the United States and in Britain (where we have seen the emergence of the Campaign against Pornography and a similar Campaign against Pornography and Censorship), some feminists, and I am one of them, (represented in Britain by the Feminists Against Censorship) passionately reject its analysis and its related practice. We see it as a mistake to reduce the dominance of sexism and misogyny in our culture to explicit representations of sexuality, whatever their nature. Men's cultural contempt for and sexualization of women long predated the growth of commercial pornography, both stemming from rather than uniquely determining the relative powerlessness of women as a sex. (Other subordinated groups are somewhat similarly sexualized and exploited, whether as Black Stud, Saphire, "effeminate" male, or working-class wanton.) Narrowing the focus on women's subordination to the explicitly sexual downplays the sexism and misogyny at work within all our most respectable social institu-

151

tions and practices, whether judicial, legal, familial, occupational, religious, scientific or cultural.

More dangerously (in today's conservative political climate) we risk terminating women's evolving exploration of our own sexuality and pleasure if we form alliances with, instead of entering the battle against, the conservative anti-pornography crusade. These are alliances which Dworkin and MacKinnon have unhesitatingly pursued in the USA, collaborating almost exclusively with the extreme Right: Presbyterian minister Mayor Hudnut III in Indianapolis, anti-ERA, anti-feminist, Republican conservative Bealah Coughenour in Minneapolis, far right preacher Greg Dixon and, of course, pro-family, anti-feminist Reagan appointee responsible for removing funds from Women's Refuges Edwin Meese. Certainly, the most effective opponents of pornography, have traditionally been, and remain, men. The men of the Moral Right (like Jesse Helms in the USA) are as deeply horrified by the feminist idea of women as sexually assertive, autonomous, and entitled to sex on their own terms, as they are by gay sex or indeed any display of the male body as the object of desire rather than the subject of authority.

Studying Pornography

Any type of blanket condemnation of pornography will discourage us all from facing up to women's own sexual fears and fantasies, which are by no means free from the guilt, anxiety, shame, contradiction, and eroticization of power on display in men's pornographic productions. And even here, those few scholars, like Linda Williams in *Hard Core*, who have chosen to study rather than make their stand over pornography, point to changes in its content which are worth studying, rather than simply dismissing. There is, to be sure, little change in the monotonous sexism of soft-core pornography. But this is increasingly *identical* with the come-on, passive, and provocative portrayal of women in advertising, or many other clearly nonpornographic genres except for the explicit crotch shot. Williams's research suggests that the most significant change in hard-core pornography (one of the few genres where women are not punished for acting out their sexual desires) is its increasing recognition of the problematic nature of sex, with clearer distinctions being made between good (consensual and safe) and bad (coercive and unsafe) sex. She attributes this shift to more women now seeing, discussing, buying, and—just occasionally—producing pornography. The changes in contemporary pornographic production mean that more women are beginning to use it. In the USA, 40 percent of "adult videos" are said to be purchased by women. Nevertheless, it is men who predominantly still produce and consume pornography, which means that it is *men's* fears and fantasies which pornography primarily addresses. (Even though more women are now hoping to enter that restricted country—if they can find the right backing and the images which turn women on.)

Uninterested in the particulars of any such shifts, the basic feminist anti-pornography argument sees all pornography as very much of a piece, and its very existence as central to the way in which men subordinate women. Pornography, in this view, both depicts and causes violence against women. Fundamental to anti-pornography feminism, most recently and comprehensively presented in Britain in Catherine Itzin's collection, *Pornography: Women, Violence and Civil Liberties*, is thus the connection made between pornography, violence, and discrimination against women. Itzin opens her collection, for example, with the claim that the U.S. Attorney General's Commission on Pornography (carefully selected by Edwin Meese III in 1985 to seek stronger law enforcement against sexually explicit images) was "unanimous in its finding of a causal link between pornography and sexual violence." In fact, as Itzin must know, there were only two feminists on the Commission, Ellen Levine and Judith Becker, both of whom rejected the Commission's findings and published their own dissenting report, claiming 'To say that exposure to pornography in and of itself causes an individual to commit a sexual crime is simplistic, not supported by the social science data, and overlooks many of the other variables that may be contributing causes."

Context Matters

Itzin's own collection, despite its numerous essays claiming to provide consistent and conclusive proof of links between pornography and violence, itself unwittingly undermines any such claim. For here, the psychologist James Weaver overturns what little consistency there was in the previous experimental data which had suggested that it was *only* sexually explicit *violent* material which could, for certain individuals, in specific laboratory conditions, be correlated with more callous responses from men towards women. Weaver's data, however, "proves" that it is exposure to any sexually explicit images, but in particular to "consensual and female instigated sex," which produces the most callous responses from men to women. It is not hard to imagine just what the conservative right might conclude using this data—from banning sex education to banning any feminist representation of sex.

What we might more reasonably conclude from the existing experimental muddle, which provides anything but clear and consistent proof of anything at all, is not really so hard to see. It is never possible, whatever the image, to isolate sexuality out, fix its meaning and predict some inevitable pattern of response, independently from assessing its wider representational context and the particular recreational, educational, or social context in which it is being received. Men together can, and regularly do, pornographize any image at all—from the Arab woman in her chador to any coding of anything as female (nuts and bolts, for example)—while the most apparently "violent" images of S & M pornography may be used in only the most consensual and caring encounters between two people. Context really does matter. This might help to explain why inconsistency is the only consistency to emerge from empirical research which ignores both the semiotic and the social context of images of sexual explicitness. As the most recent Home Office report on pornography commissioned in the UK concluded: "inconsistencies emerge between very similar studies and many interpretations of these have reached almost opposite conclusions."

Women's Experience of Harm

Some anti-pornography feminists who are more aware of both the inconsistency and possible irrelevance of the experimental proof of pornography's harm have preferred to call upon the testimony of women's own experience of the harm they feel pornography has caused them. A typical example is the evidence provided by one woman at the Minneapolis public hearings. There she described how, after reading *Playboy*, *Penthouse* and *Forum*, her husband developed an interest in group sex, took her to various pornographic institutions and even invited a friend into their marital bed. To prevent any further group situations occurring, which she found very painful, this woman had agreed to act out in private scenarios depicting bondage and the different sex acts which her husband wanted her to perform, even though she found them all very humiliating. It was only after learning karate and beginning to travel on her own that this woman could feel strong enough to leave her husband. This is indeed moving testimony, but surely all along there was only one suitable solution to any such woman's distress: having the power and confidence to leave a man, or any person, who forced her into actions she wished to avoid, and who showed no concern for her own wishes. Pornography is not the problem here, nor is its elimination the solution.

Another type of gruesome evidence frequently used by anti-pornography feminists to establish links between pornography and violence draws upon the myth of the "snuff movie," first circulated in New York in 1975, about underground films supposedly coming from South America in which women were murdered on camera apparently reaching a sexual climax. On investigation such movies, like the classic film *Snuff* itself, released in the U.S. in 1976, have always turned out to be a variant of the slasher film, using the special effects of the horror genre, and thus distinct from what is seen as the genre of pornography. There is, however, also the personal testimony of some former sex workers, exemplified by that of Linda Lovelace Marchiano. Linda Marchiano in her book *Ordeal* has described how she was coerced, bullied, and beaten by her husband, Chuck Traynor, into working as a porn actress. (Interestingly, however, although coerced into sex work by a violent husband, the book actually describes how it was her success as a porn actress in *Deep Throat* which gave Linda Traynor the confidence to leave her husband, re-marry, and start campaigning for "respectable family life" and against pornography.)

The more general problem here is that other sex workers complain bitterly about what they see as the false and hypocritical victimization of them by anti-pornography feminists, whose campaigns they believe, if successful, would serve only to worsen their pay and working conditions, and increase the stigmatization of their work. (I am not referring here, of course, to the production of child pornography, which is illegal, along with other forms of exploitation of children.) Some sex workers declare that they choose and like the work they do, and the type of control they believe it gives them over their lives. Indeed, it has been suggested that the feminist anti-pornography campaign itself primarily reflects the privileges of largely white and middle-class women who, not being as exploited as many other women, can self-servingly present the issue of women's sexual objectification by men as the source of oppression of all women.

Power, Not Porn, Is the Problem

Whether it is from abused women or abused sex workers, however, what we hear when we do hear, or read, women's testimony against pornography or the pornography industry are stories of women coercively pressured into sex, or sexual display, which they do not want—varying from straight to oral, anal, bondage, and group sex. But we would be more than foolish if we saw the harm we were hearing about as residing in the pornographic images themselves, or in the possibility of enacting them (all, without any doubt, practices which certain women as well as men, at certain times, freely choose), and not in the men's (or possibly, although very rarely in heterosexual encounters, women's) abuse of power. The harm, it is important we should be clear, is contained not in the explicitly sexual material, but in the social context which deprives a woman (or sometimes a man) of her (or his) ability to reject any unwanted sexual activity—whether with husband, lover, parent, relative, friend, acquaintance, or stranger. And this is one fundamental reason feminists opposed to anti-pornography campaigning are so distressed at each attempt to bring in some new version of the Minneapolis Ordinance, like the so-called Pornography Victims' Compensation Act first introduced into the U.S. Senate in 1989, and cropping up again in New York, in 1992, or Itzin's own proposals taken up by MPs [members of Parliament] like Dawn Primarolo and Clare Short in Britain.

It is not just that these bills, quite contrary to the self-deceiving rhetoric of their advocates (Itzin and Dworkin claim to be "absolutely opposed to censorship in every form") would suppress sexual and erotic materials by opening up the threat of quite unprecedented levels of censorship through harassing lawsuits and financial penalties against producers, distributors, booksellers, writers, photographers, and movie makers. It is also that, again quite contrary to the stated goals of their supporters, such legislative proposals cost nothing and do nothing to provide real remedies against men's violence. State funding for women's refuges, anti-sexist, anti-violence educational initiatives, and above all empowering women more fundamentally through improved job prospects, housing, and welfare facilities, would seem to be the only effective ways of enabling women to avoid violence.

Removing Blame

Instead, however, the idea that pornographic material causes men's violence tends to excuse the behavior of the men who are sexually coercive and violent, by removing the blame on to pornography. Men who rape, murder, and commit other violent sex crimes against women, children or other men may (or may not) have an interest in violent pornography. However, as overviews of all the available empirical data suggest, the evidence does not point to pornography as a cause of their behavior.

When Itzin, along with so many of the authors in her collection, weirdly but repeatedly cite as "evidence" for pornography's harm the final testimony of serial killer Ted Bundy before his execution, they surely do more to expose rather than to support their argument. Today both the rapist and, even more hypocritically, tabloid wisdom have learnt to lay the blame for sex crimes on "pornography" (whereas once, with the same sort of certainty, they would lay the blame on "mothers").

Meanwhile, although Dworkin, MacKinnon, Itzin, and their supporters continue to argue that it is pornography which violates women's civil rights by increasing discrimination against them, studies in the USA and Europe have tended to reverse the picture. In the U.S. it is in states with a preponderance of Southern Baptists (followers of leading anti-pornography campaigner Jerry Falwell) that the highest levels of social, political, and economic inequality between women and men can be found despite the lowest circulation of pornography. Indeed Larry Baron discovered a positive correlation between equal opportunities for women in employment, education and politics, and higher rates of pornography which he attributed to the greater social tolerance generally in these states. Such findings are consistent with those from Europe, where we find far higher levels of overall economic, political, and other indices of gender equality in Sweden and Denmark compared to either the USA or Britain, and lower levels of violence against women—coupled with more liberal attitudes towards pornography. Baron's survey, interestingly, also found that gender inequality correlated with the presence and extent of legitimate use of violence in a state (as measured by the numbers of people trained to work in the military, the use of corporal punishment in schools, government use of violence—as in the death penalty), as well as with mass media preferences for violence, as in circulation rates of *Guns and Ammo*).

Beyond Pornography

It is time for feminists, and their supporters, who want to act against men's greater use of violence and sexual coercion, and against men's continuing social dominance, to abandon anti-pornography feminism. . . .

In the end, anti-pornography campaigns, feminist or not, can only enlist today, as they invariably enlisted before, centuries of guilt and anxiety around sex, as well as lifetimes of confusion and complexity in our personal experiences of sexual arousal and activity. In contrast, campaigns which get to the heart of men's violence and sadism towards women must enlist the widest possible resources to empower women socially to seek only the types of sexual encounters they choose, and to empower women sexually to explore openly their own interests and pleasures. We do need the space to produce our own sexually explicit narratives and images of female desire and sensuous engagement if we are even to begin to embark upon that journey.

VIEWPOINT

"Even so-called nonviolent material . . . makes men more likely to see women as less than human, . . . and unequal to men."

Feminists Should Oppose Pornography's Harmful Effects

Alice Leuchtag

In the following viewpoint, Alice Leuchtag presents the views of a number of feminists who believe that the institutions of the sex industry—including prostitution and pornography—are among the forces that sustain women's inferiority to men in social status, power, and wealth. Specifically, Leuchtag summarizes the arguments of Catharine A. MacKinnon, who argues that pornography teaches men to view and treat women as sexual objects, thereby keeping them in a subordinate position. Leuchtag concludes that these feminists are correct to oppose the production and use of pornography. Leuchtag holds a B.A. in psychology and sociology from the University of California at Los Angeles and an M.A. in sociology from San Diego State University.

As you read, consider the following questions:

1. According to Jane Anthony, as cited by the author, what causes some women to become prostitutes?
2. How is "woman" defined, according to Catharine MacKinnon, as quoted by Leuchtag?
3. What should be the humanist position on prostitution and pornography, in Leuchtag's opinion?

Alice Leuchtag, "The Culture of Pornography," *Humanist,* May/June 1995. Reprinted with permission of the author.

Despite many gains in the latter part of the twentieth century, women as a group are still clearly inferior to men in status, power, knowledge, and wealth. As a result, many unresolved ethical issues still exist in the relationship between the sexes. Two of the thorniest of these are prostitution and pornography.

Diminishing the Lives of Women

Many great feminists of the past considered the institution of prostitution as central to an understanding of the socially subordinate position of women. These individuals include essayist and historian Mary Wollstonecraft, poet and novelist Olive Schreiner, political activist and anarchist Emma Goldman, writer and suffragist Charlotte Perkins Gilman, and economist and sociologist Victoria Woodhull—to mention only a few of the most notable.

This concern about a very old institution has carried over into the present day, both in the work of feminist scholars and in the debates that are taking place within the women's liberation movement. Even though there is a minority of women who defend prostitution and other work in the sex industry as a legitimate career choice, many women—even some who would not label themselves as feminist—feel that the sex industry in general, and the institution of prostitution in particular, diminishes the lives of the women who work in it, as well as diminishing the general status of all women. Yet there are differences as to what changes can and should be made within the constraints posed by our constitutional system.

Activist scholar, teacher, and writer Jane Anthony, in her article "Prostitution As 'Choice'" (*Ms.*, January/February 1992), points out that, traditionally, prostitution has been considered a necessary evil that helps to preserve the institution of marriage by providing a readily available outlet for men's sexual desires. To illustrate this attitude, Anthony quotes from Thomas Aquinas, who wrote that "prostitution is like a sewer system, despicable but necessary." As Anthony points out, Aquinas' view overlooks the fact that there are casualties in the system brought about by the fact that "one class of women is granted status as wives or girlfriends at the expense of another class, whores, who are reduced to sperm receptacles for numerous men."

Some recent literature, written by women who consider themselves feminists, has presented a pro-prostitution stance in which prostitution is portrayed as a "career choice." Anthony maintains that pro-prostitution ideology, often considered sexual liberalism, reflects a dualism in which nineteenth-century views of prostitutes as victims are set off against current views of prostitutes as women who make active decisions to become whores. According to Anthony, only if commercial sex is decontextualized from the social and cultural forces that constrict women's choices—such as job discrimination, gender inequality in the courts, and a "sexism so pervasive it is often invisible"—can prostitution be seen as a choice. Thus, says Anthony, "in decontextualizing women's choices, pro-prostitution ideology inadvertently trivializes prostitution."

Anthony also calls into question those who see prostitution as a form of empowerment for women. She maintains that this may be true temporarily for those women who have been sexually abused prior to becoming prostitutes (and these constitute a large percentage of prostitutes, according to Anthony) and for whom a sense of empowerment exists relative to their previous abuse. Still, under conditions of prostitution, a sense of empowerment is transitory and illusory, Anthony maintains. She states that she speaks from personal experience, having worked as a prostitute for several years. She also quotes Evelina Giobbe of Women Hurt in Systems of Prostitution Engaged in Revolt (WHISPER), who says: "Dismantling the institution of prostitution is the most formidable task facing contemporary feminism."

Feminists Should Oppose Prostitution

In a more academic vein is philosopher Laurie Shrage, who contributed an article to the anthology *Feminism and Political Theory* entitled "Should Feminists Oppose Prostitution?" Declaring that "prostitution raises difficult issues for feminists," Shrage asks whether or not persons opposed to the social subordination of women should seek to discourage commercial sex. Her answer is emphatically yes. Shrage focuses her arguments on what must be done to subvert widely held beliefs that legitimize prostitution in our society, because once these beliefs are undermined, "nothing closely resembling prostitution, as we currently know it, will exist."

Shrage, like Anthony, considers prostitution within its cultural context. She declares that "it epitomizes and perpetuates pernicious patriarchal beliefs and values, and, therefore, is both damaging to the women who sell sex and, as an organized social practice, to all women in our society." She also argues that it reinforces certain cultural assumptions which give legitimacy to women's social subordination, including the belief that men are naturally suited for dominant social roles and the belief that a person's sexual practice defines him or her as a particular kind of person (for example, a "homosexual" a "whore" a "virgin" or a "pervert").

In Shrage's view, the principles that organize and sustain the sex industry are the same ones that underlie many other pernicious and oppressive gender asymmetries in our social institutions. She concludes:

I am unable to imagine nonpernicious principles which would legitimate the commercial provision of sex and which would not substantially alter or eliminate the industry as it now exists. Since commercial sex, unlike marriage, is not reformable, feminists should seek to undermine the beliefs and values which underlie our acceptance of it. Indeed, one way to do this is to outwardly oppose prostitution itself. . . . In this respect, a consumer boycott of the sex industry is especially appropriate.

There is a close historical connection between pornography and prostitution. (The word *pornography* itself means, quite literally, "writing about prostitutes.") Along with the concern and debate over prostitution, then, an even fiercer debate is raging in the current women's movement over pornography.

The name most prominently associated with the abolitionist view regarding pornography is Catharine A. MacKinnon, professor of law at the University of Michigan Law School. In her own contribution to *Feminism and Political Theory*, entitled "Sexuality, Pornography, and Method: Pleasure Under Patriarchy," MacKinnon focuses on the processes by which the social subordination of women to men is accomplished and maintained under patriarchy—processes in which, she claims, the learning and practice of a sexuality of dominance and submission play a crucial role. To MacKinnon, pornography is one of the ways in which the system of dominance and submission is maintained, a system whose underlying dynamic depends on the sexual objectification of women. MacKinnon places the dehumanization of women along a continuum of female submission—from visual appropriation of the female in pornography, to physical appropriation in prostituted sex, to forced sex in rape, to sexual murder.

MacKinnon cites many recent feminist studies on rape, battery, sexual harassment, sexual abuse of children, prostitution, and pornography that point out specific mechanisms of sexual objectification. According to MacKinnon, when pornography is seen as part of a totality of mutually reinforcing sex practices, it both symbolizes and actualizes the distinctive social power that men as a class have over women as a class in patriarchal society. To quote MacKinnon:

> In feminist terms, the fact that male power has power means that the interests of male sexuality construct what sexuality as such means in life, including the standard way it is allowed and recognized to be felt and expressed and experienced. A theory of sexuality becomes feminist to the extent that it treats sexuality as a social construct of male power: defined by men, forced on women, and constitutive in the meaning of gender. Existing theories, until they grasp this, will not only misattribute what they call female sexuality to women as such, as if it is not imposed on women daily, they will participate in enforcing the hegemony of the social construct "desire" hence its product, "sexuality" hence its construct "woman" on the world.

The gender issue thus becomes the issue of what is taken to be "sexuality": what sex means and what is meant by sex, when, how, and with whom and with what consequences to whom.

Such questions are almost never systematically confronted, even in discourses that purport feminist awareness. Feminist theory becomes, then, a project of analyzing that situation in order to face it for what it is, in order to change it.

Women as Objects

Thus, MacKinnon sees pornography as one of the primary means by which women are made into sexual objects: "First in the world, then in the head, first in visual appropriation, then in forced sex, finally in sexual murder. . . ." It is partly through the means of pornography itself, claims MacKinnon, that the gender qualities we know culturally as "male" and "female" are socially created and enforced in everyday life.

Like Anthony and Shrage, MacKinnon sees human sexuality not as a given of nature but as a construct of a specific culture, conditioned in both women and men by the ubiquitous existence of gender inequality in a patriarchal culture. To MacKinnon, being a thing for sexual use is fundamental to the content of sexuality for women under patriarchy:

> Specifically, "woman" is defined by what male desire requires for arousal and satisfaction and is socially tautologous with "female sexuality" and "the female sex." . . . To be clear: what is sexual is what gives a man an erection. Whatever it takes to make a penis shudder and stiffen with the experience of its potency is what sexuality means culturally.

To the question, "What do men want?" MacKinnon notes:

> Pornography provides an answer. . . . From the testimony of the pornography, what men want is: women bound, women battered, women tortured, women humiliated, women degraded and defiled, women killed, or, to be fair to the soft core, women sexually accessible, have-able, there for them, wanting to be taken and used, with perhaps just a little light bondage.

To buttress this point, MacKinnon cites experimental data on pornography which, she claims, substantiates the connection between gender inequality, pornography, and male sexuality. When "normal" men in a laboratory setting view pornography over time, they become more aroused by scenes of rape than by scenes of explicit (but not expressly violent) sex, even if the woman is shown as hating it. Apparently, sustained perceptual exposure to pornography inures subjects to the violent component in overtly violent sexual material, while increasing the arousal value of such material. Experimental studies also show that viewing sexual material containing explicit aggression against women makes normal men more willing to aggress against women, as well as more likely to see a woman rape victim as less human and more blameworthy. Even so-called nonviolent material in which women are verbally abused, dominated, or treated as sexual toys makes men more likely to see women as less than human, good only for sex, blameworthy when raped, and unequal to men.

MacKinnon, Shrage, and Anthony, as representative modern feminist scholars, agree that specific forces in our patriarchal culture create and maintain a hierarchy of gender in which the social institutions of prostitution and pornography can flourish. None of the three believes there is an innate human sexuality as such, unconditioned by specific cultures, although at times MacKinnon seems to forget her basic premise and writes about male sexuality as if it is a natural, unconditioned given, outside of culture.

These three writers also agree that feminists cannot ignore these issues, difficult as they are with their many legal, political, and social ramifications. They take to task those people who defend prostitution or the pornography industry as legitimate career choices for women. They maintain that, overall, women who work in these areas are exploited and demeaned, that their civil rights are frequently trampled upon, and that they face severe physical and psychological risks. While not blaming the victim for being a victim, all three writers are searching, both theoretically and practically, for ways in which these institutions can be altered or abolished. To accomplish such formidable tasks within the constitutional framework of law is seen by these writers and by many other feminists as primary among the compelling ethical, legal, and political challenges facing the women's movement in the twenty-first century.

What should the humanist position be on those questions? I think this depends on which aspect of the humanist movement one considers most important: the free-thought, skeptical, liberal current of humanism; or the (in my opinion) far deeper current that humanism shares with certain other philosophical traditions—namely, concern for the welfare and betterment of humanity. If concern for humanity's welfare is considered as foremost in humanism, then attitudes of skepticism and liberality are viewed as a means to an end rather than as ends in themselves. They are employed where useful (for example, to critique religious dogma) but not revered on general principles. Skepticism and liberalism need not hobble us in the face of pernicious social institutions. If one stresses humanity's welfare, prostitution and pornography would have to be viewed as giant-sized stumbling blocks to human progress, inasmuch as they demean one class of humans by converting them into commercial objects.

"What's important . . . isn't just that I learned how to get physically aroused by pornography but that I became sexually autonomous. I was now in complete control of my own erotic destiny."

Feminists Should Embrace Pornography's Liberating Effects

Lisa Palac

Lisa Palac is the former editor of San Francisco's *Cybersex* magazine and the creator of the CD-ROM program *Cyborgasm*. In the following viewpoint, Palac writes that viewing pornography improved her sexual life and caused her to change from an anti-pornography feminist to the editor of a pornographic magazine. Palac believes that pornography can help women gain control over their own sexuality and can thereby assist them in their movement for freedom and social justice.

As you read, consider the following questions:

1. When does the author say she first questioned her anti-pornography stance?
2. How did pornography improve her erotic imagination, according to Palac?
3. What problems does the author say she now has with the views of anti-pornography feminists?

From "How Dirty Pictures Changed My Life," by Lisa Palac, copyright © 1994 by Lisa Palac, from *Next: Young American Writers on the New Generation*, edited by Eric Liu. Reprinted by permission of W.W. Norton & Company, Inc.

"Burn it," I said. The words clinked together like ice cubes. "Burn every last bit of it. Or it's over."

I pointed at the stockpile of hard-core porn that had just slid out of the closet like an avalanche. If looks could kill, my boyfriend would have dropped dead. How could he, Mr. Sensitive Guy, enjoy looking at such disgusting trash? Oh, I was livid. I paced around his tiny one-room apartment, spitting venom, devising his punishment. "Either all this sleazy shit goes or I go."

He looked at me as if he were about to cry; his fingers nervously picked at the edges of his flannel shirt. "I'll get rid of it all, I promise," he whispered. Silence fell around the room like a metal drape. "But first will you watch one—just one—video with me?" The nerve. Here I am threatening to walk, and he's got the audacity to ask me to watch a fuck film before I go. He prattled on about how he just wanted a chance to show me why this stuff turned him on and that it didn't mean he didn't love me and if I didn't like it, he would, as agreed, torch everything in a purging bonfire. I crossed my arms and chewed on the inside of my lip for a minute. If I was going to make him destroy his life's collection of porn, I guess I could allow him one last fling. So that evening we watched *Sleepless Nights*. It was the first dirty movie I ever saw. A seminal film.

Good Girls Didn't Look at Porn

I saw that movie when I was twenty years old, and now I'm twenty-nine. Since then I've watched hundreds of X-rated videos, patronized plenty of erotic theaters, put money down for live sex shows, and even run up a few phone-sex bills. Today I make my living making porn. I edit an erotic magazine titled *Future Sex* and recently produced the virtual-reality-based sex CD-ROM program *Cyborgasm*. I've always been a firm believer that if you want something done right, you've got to do it yourself.

Until I sat down and watched an adult film, the only thing I knew about porn was that I shouldn't be looking at it. Growing up female, I quickly learned that girls don't get to look at girlie magazines. Sure, you could take your clothes off for the camera (becoming, of course, a total slut and disgracing your family), but the pleasure is for *his* eyes only. The message to us girls was, Stay a virgin until you get married, procreate, and don't bother finding your clitoris. Whatever you do, stay away from porn, because it's a man's world, honey. Ironically certain strains of feminism gave a similar sermon: Pornography can only exploit, oppress, and degrade you. It will destroy any female in its path, unless you can destroy it first. And if you don't believe this, you've obviously been brainwashed by The Patriarchy.

If the truth be known, the forbidden aspect of pornography made me a little curious. However, I wasn't about to be caught renting a porn video. So when Greg challenged me to watch an X-rated movie, I decided to see for myself what all the fuss was about.

At the time, I thought of myself as an antiporn feminist. . . .

Minneapolis [where I was attending school] was a hotbed of radical antiporn politics. Catharine MacKinnon and Andrea Dworkin were teaching a class on porn at the University of Minnesota, and they drafted the very first feminist-inspired antipornography law, defining pornography as a form of sex discrimination. *The Story of O* was picketed on campus, with flyers denouncing S&M as just another bourgeois word for violence. *Not a Love Story*, a documentary about one woman's adverse experience in the adult business, had become a women's-studies classic. One woman set herself on fire in Shinder's Bookstore on Hennepin Avenue, a martyr for the right to a porn-free society. The message was clear: This battle was as important as ending the Vietnam War.

Pornography for Women

Women deserve to create their own sexuality. But the way to do that just might be to give women a pornography of their own, available to them when their curiosity begins to develop. Not watered-down erotica or Harlequin romances. Not *Playgirl*'s polite hunks, and certainly not *Playboy*'s passive centerfolds. Adolescent girls need sexy magazines that are passed along by their sisters and given as gift subscriptions by maiden aunts, with nudges and winks all around. Magazines that encourage them to look without shame at dirty pictures. Some feminists would like to dictate women's sexual tastes, but such tastes are rich and varied and they aren't always politically correct. A man can buy pornography that caters to every fantasy under the sun. Women deserve the same. . . .

In pornography's power to arouse lies its potential for good as well as harm. It allows adolescents to explore the unsettling feelings occasioned by the opposite sex (or the same sex, if that's their pleasure) in the safety of their own bedrooms.

Celia Barbour, *New York Times*, April 23, 1994.

Meanwhile the Meese Commission [which was established by Ronald Reagan in 1984] was in full swing, bringing *Deep Throat* star Linda "Lovelace" Marchiano's disturbing testimony of coercion into the living rooms of America and alleging a link between pornography and violence. Women Against Pornography toured the heartland with their slide show, featuring the infamous *Hus-*

tler cover of a woman being fed through a meat grinder. The tenet seemed to be this: Get rid of porn and get rid of all injustice against women. All the battles feminists were fighting could be won by winning the war on porn. So I enlisted.

I didn't have any firsthand experience with porn. I had never watched an adult film, bought an explicit sex magazine, or known anyone who did. Aside from a few stolen glances at my father's collection, the only pornography I saw was in the classroom. This carefully selected group of pornographic images didn't appear very liberating. . . . These images were described as inherently degrading and oppressive. No other interpretation was offered. I looked at these images (which were supposedly representative of all porn), added my own experience of being sized up as a piece of ass, and agreed that pornography was the reason women were oppressed. Pornography bred sexism. Like Justice Potter Stewart, I knew pornography when I saw it and I'd seen enough to swallow the rally cries of the antiporn movement. I chanted and marched and applauded the spray painting of LIES ABOUT WOMEN over Virginia Slims ads and across the fronts of XXX black-veiled bookstores. I learned the slogans like "Porn is the theory and rape is the practice" from older feminists like Robin Morgan.

Sex and Sexism

But soon I began to wonder how it all fit in with what I was doing in my bedroom. I still liked men, even if I didn't like all their piggish behavior. And I liked sleeping with them even more. Since I was fifteen, I used my feminine charms to lure them in. They used their virility to seduce me. Did this constitute sexual objectification? I wasn't sure. I questioned the definition of pornography I'd been handed. Yes, the images I'd seen offended me, but surely there were sexual images that weren't sexist. Where were the erotic alternatives? If the bottom line here was that looking at images of people having sex was wrong, then I hadn't come very far from Catholic school after all. Plus, lumping all men under the heading Sexist Patriarchy seemed a little unfair. The guys I hung out with were caring, respectful, and intelligent—but could they suddenly turn into psychopathic rapists if I waved a porn mag in front of their faces? Underneath it all, I had a lot of questions. And then my boyfriend's porn came tumbling out of the closet. . . .

Alone with Pornography

I made an important decision: I decided I needed to be alone with pornography. I wondered what might turn me on—if anything. . . . I wanted to perform an experiment, to watch it by myself without him, without talking. I could no longer scrutinize these images from an intellectual distance. I had to get a little dirty.

I made a date with an "all-lesbian" action feature called *Aerobisex Girls*. I tried not to care about the plot. I didn't wonder about the performers' family histories. I didn't think about anything. The movie featured an oiled-up orgy where the women shook with the fury of real, uncontrollable orgasms. . . . I opened and closed my eyes, imagining I was part of their scene, replaying certain close-ups over and over. Then my mind began moving back and forth between the real-time video and the frozen frames of cherished erotic memories. I fed the screen with my own fantasies, splicing together an erotic sequence that played only in my head. When I came, it was intense. . . .

Enhancing One's Erotic Imagination

At the beginning of my porn adventures, I was confused. I was looking for a political theory instead of a sexual experience, and that's why it hadn't been working. Now I had the carnal knowledge that so few women possessed: how to use porn and come. What's important about this isn't just that I learned how to get physically aroused by pornography but that I became sexually autonomous. I was now in complete control of my own erotic destiny. My experience was sexual liberation in action. I now knew how to use my mind to turn a two-dimensional image into a flesh-and-blood erotic response and explore sexual fantasies.

Before I watched porn, my erotic imagination was groggy. I didn't know what a sexual fantasy was; I hadn't really had them. Even when I masturbated, I didn't think about anything except the physical sensations. When I had sex with my lovers, my thoughts were filled only with them, the way they were touching me, the immediacy of the act. And that was good. But there were all these other thoughts that I hadn't explored yet. Pornography dangled sexual fantasy in front of me. It made me aware that my sexual imagination wasn't limited to the heat of the moment or a sensual reminiscence. I could think about *anything*. I could use *anything*—books, magazines, videos—for erotic inspiration. . . .

Much to my relief my female friends were extremely supportive. They related to my journey from antiporn feminism to sex-positive feminism, because many of them were on the same trip. They, too, were fed up with everyone shouting, "Don't look!" when it came to porn. They wanted to see it and they wanted me to show it to them. My friend Bitsy even asked me to invite all the girls over for pizza and porno night.

As we talked, I realized that learning how to use porn is an option most women are never aware of. Too many women only react to pornography as a political debate. Pornography, erotica, sexography, whatever you choose to call it, is a tangled genre with a few razor-sharp sides. This complexity is a reflection of the mystery and depth of our own sexuality, where erotic conflict often makes for excitement. My investigation into the erotic world has resulted in a few mixed feelings. There were images that troubled me, and there still are. But I believe my initial knee-jerk reaction against porn was a result of my own misunderstanding and lack of sensitivity to erotic images.

Pornography as a whole is usually described as offensive. Yet I found that much of what is offensive about porn has to do with interpretations, not sexual acts. . . .

The words *degrading* and *oppressive* are often presented as absolute, objective terms. I found them to be vague and subjective. Was the very act of a woman spreading her legs and wanting sex degrading? Were photographs of her genitals outright demeaning? Why is the image of a woman's sexual appetite seen as oppressive rather than liberating? If we're going to talk about oppressive images of women, we'd better include laundry soap commercials. The depiction of women as vapid Stepford wives, valued only for their stain-removing talents, is to me completely oppressive.

Another thing that really surprised me as I explored this erotic underworld was the lack of violent porn. I was taught to believe that all porn was violent. However, my own exploration quickly revealed that the majority of commercial porn is rather peacefully formulaic. No knives, no blood, no rape scenes. Instead there was a . . . formula that ended in orgasm, not murder.

Ultimately I felt the antiporn feminists viewed women as being without sexual self-awareness. Their arguments for the elimination of porn were shaky and flawed. Their claims denied women independence by refusing to acknowledge that women had rich sexual fantasies, powerful libidos, and the power to choose. . . .

More and more women are realizing that erotic images have a necessary place in their lives. Sexual freedom is an integral part of freedom and justice for all. If the basic tenet of feminism is giving women the freedom to choose, then it includes making choices about what we do sexually.

5

"A real danger exists that antiporn ideology actually promotes *the attitudes that lead to sexual violence."*

Anti-Pornography Feminists Harm the Women's Movement

Avedon Carol

Avedon Carol, a founding member of Feminists Against Censorship, serves on the executive committee of *Liberty*, a monthly libertarian magazine. She is coeditor of the book *Bad Girls and Dirty Pictures: The Challenge to Reclaim Feminism* and the author of *Nudes, Prudes, and Attitudes: Pornography and Censorship*. In the following viewpoint, Carol expresses her opinion that the anti-pornography feminist movement threatens the advancement of women. Feminists who want to "protect" women from pornography are simply restricting women's freedom, she writes, and ultimately harming the very women they aim to help.

As you read, consider the following questions:

1. What political alliance have anti-pornography feminists made that the author finds frightening?
2. How does free sexual expression affect gender roles, in Carol's opinion?
3. Instead of pornography, what problems should feminists focus on, in the author's opinion?

Avedon Carol, "Free Speech and the Porn Wars." Reprinted from *National Forum: The Phi Kappa Phi Journal*, vol. 75, no. 2 (Spring 1995), copyright © by Avedon Carol, by permission of the publishers.

Under the circumstances, pornography could be restricted under obscenity laws because it was alleged to have no political content of any kind and therefore was not "expression" as such. Even as restrictions on sexual material were being lifted in the 1950s and 1960s, and social science had begun to take a less negative view of masturbation, pornography was still seen as, at best, "empty calories."

Feminists generally had a negative view of pornography, partly because we felt that it pandered to the lowest and least edifying aspects of male sexuality and partly because we perceived its content as being largely sexist. Some also felt that pornographic materials promoted an idealized standard of female beauty with which real women could not compete.

On the other hand, feminists also were aware that legislation restricting sexual content always became a weapon against feminist speech as well as other material meant to create, either in art or explicitly political expression, a challenge to the status quo. Because sexual content was deemed sordid and without merit, obscenity movements and laws had been the tools that suppressed some aspects of Black culture—at one point, the blues were banned in Memphis itself—and also information promoting reproductive health. For example, Margaret Sanger was arrested under obscenity laws for telling women about birth control. As the modern women's liberation movement emerged in the late 1960s and early 1970s, a spate of obscenity actions were directed at feminist materials; *Ms.* magazine, the healthcare handbook *Our Bodies, Our Selves*, and Judy Grahan's poetry were typical targets.

Antipornography Feminism

Overall, feminists were anti-censorship virtually by definition, until the advent of antipornography feminism. Although most long-time feminists still opposed censorship, by the late 1980s the media were presenting a view of the pornography debate that placed feminists directly in opposition to the First Amendment. This image was encouraged by the high visibility of campaigns by Andrea Dworkin and Catharine MacKinnon, and also by America's premier feminist magazine, *Ms.*, taking the antipornography position at the editorial level.

For many feminists, however, the antipornography, pro-censorship view represented a return to pre-feminist consciousness. The language of antiporn women, whether on the right or left, was largely judgmental of sex and of women in much the same way as might have been found in social-purity tracts. The view of gender roles these activists expressed was and is explicitly one that glories in the sex dualism and fully stereotypes males and females along the sugar-and-spice/snakes-and-snails model in which the "bestial" urges of the male must be counteracted and controlled by the motherly purity of the female.

Perhaps most importantly, antipornography feminism rests wholly on a desexualized model of femaleness—what once was known as "femininity." Reactionary feminists, as Gayle Rubin noted in her speech to the National Organization for Women's pornography hearings, "Misguided, Dangerous, and Wrong" (a version of which can be found in *Bad Girls & Dirty Pictures*, edited by A. Assiter & A. Carol), had been using terminology that specifically debased sex workers. Moreover, those with long memories and some knowledge of feminist history recognized the essential pro-sex factor at the foundation of every known feminist movement in history.

Pawns of the Moral Right

And those with a keen eye and a fully developed feminist consciousness could not help but notice that an alliance was being forged between antiporn feminists and the most thoroughly antifeminist members of the moral right. In America, this alliance was made chillingly obvious in the Meese Commission hearings. [The Meese Commission was established in 1984 by President Ronald Reagan to investigate the link between pornography and violence.] As Carole S. Vance pointed out in "Negotiating Sex and Gender in the Attorney General's Commission on Pornography" (in *Sex Exposed*, edited by Lynne Segal & Mary McIntosh, from Virago Press, London, 1992), the language of "feminists" was easily adapted to the world view of longtime antifeminist campaigners. Indeed, the right-wing repressives were visibly winning the war in terms of *how* antiporn rhetoric would be interpreted and used. And despite the optimism Andrea Dworkin and her colleagues expressed to the press, it was clear from the outset that "feminists" were mere pawns in the furtherance of a repressive, right-wing agenda.

What is clear, however, is that pornography has ceased to be inert as the argument has gone on. Liberals, libertarians, and feminists have all accepted the idea that free sexual expression plays an important part in permitting a discourse that challenges traditional gender roles. This function, of course, is why the moral right always has objected to pornography, a point that becomes explicit in their more recent writings on the subject.

Perhaps the greatest irony in the debate is the frequent citation by antiporn feminists of antiporn researcher Dolf Zillmann. Zillmann is responsible for convincing people that pornography makes men "callous toward women," by which he means that pornography encourages men to question traditional sex roles; Zillmann's work makes abundantly clear that he considers it "callous" to treat women as anything more than baby-making machines and receptacles for *male* sexuality.

The writings and speeches of antiporn "feminists" such as Dworkin, MacKinnon, and Sheila Jeffreys work along remarkably similar lines. The frequent charge they make against pornography is that it "misrepresents" women by showing us as enjoying sexual activity. In works such as *Anticlimax* (Jeffreys), *Pornography: Men Possessing Women,* and *Intercourse* (Dworkin), and in numerous speeches, these women have promoted the view that women are uniformly disgusted and harmed by sexual experimentation and pornography. And, although they try to paint their opponents as being merely "pro-porn," our disagreements are much more fundamental: we cannot agree that women have *any* uniform view or experience of sex and pornography. As long-time feminists, we cannot participate in this kind of stereotyping of women, let alone the attendant stereotyping of men and sexuality that comes with the package.

Women and Pornography

In fact, many women enjoy sex and pornography, and many others probably are put off more by sexist assumptions than by anything inherent in pornography or sex itself. If women are persistently being told that we can only be "used" in sex, it can be difficult for many of us to relax and explore our own responses unhindered. If we are constantly told that sexually explicit media can appeal only to men, our sense of exclusion may override our ability to examine sexual media openly.

The true feminist criticism of pornography is the criticism of the media and society in general:

• It continues to suppress a more open, honest, and diverse exploration of gender and of sexuality (see almost anything on network television or coming out of Hollywood in the mainstream), thus leaving explicit representations of sex isolated in the dark corners of porn shops.

• It persists in holding to dangerous and offensive stereotypes (such as can be found in *Fatal Attraction* and *Basic Instinct*).

• The stigmatization of sexuality for women makes us particularly vulnerable to harassment and abuse (which is just as true in factories and offices, but less likely to engender sympathy when we are in the sex industry).

Ironically, pornography is actually *less* likely to stereotype women in the ways that are common to the rest of the culture; for example, pornography is still the only genre that does not pass judgment against women for being sexual, as Linda Williams noted in *Hard Core*. In pornography, it would be completely unacceptable for a man to react with violence to catching his wife in bed with someone else. And a far greater variety of female types are shown as desirable in pornography than mainstream film and network television have ever recognized: fat women, flat women, hairy women, aggressive women, older women, you name it. Pornography actually offers a more realistic view of women's diversity—and desirability—than can be found in any other genre, including feminist media.

The Same Old Censorship

Pro-censorship feminists, personified by Andrea Dworkin and Catharine MacKinnon, argue . . . that "pornography"—as they very broadly define it—is central to women's oppression, that it is action not speech, that its very existence violates women's rights. . . . A large and growing number of women—especially feminists who are writers, artists, scholars, critics, and intellectuals—are scornful of suggestions that censorship is the remedy for violence against women. . . . They understand that suppression brings the same old efforts to control women's bodies, women's sexuality, women's lives.

Leanne Katz, *Crossroads*, March 1993.

Some feminists say that they accept nonsexist erotic media, however explicit, and distinguish this from *pornography*. Because the term pornography generally is recognized as referring to sexual media, rather than to sexist media, this rather begs the question of why such feminists use this word at all; certainly the dictionaries do not use words referring to exploitation, sexism, and violence in their definitions of the term. People go to porn shops looking for sexual materials, not for "sexist" materials. Similarly, people who make and sell pornography understand themselves to be selling sexual materials, not violent, exploitative, or sexist materials. Traditional antiporn campaigners have always complained of sex, not sexism, in pornography.

Pornography and Violence

When Catharine MacKinnon came to England to promote her book *Only Words* she told an interviewer on television's *The Late Show* that by pornography she meant what was on the market, what was generally available. Yet a few minutes later she said that pornography meant material that was degrading, violent, or represented the torture of women. In the book itself, she claims to be talking about the sexually explicit media that are generally available and popular with men (she denied on *The Late Show* and also on David Frost's show that women liked pornography at all), yet she refers only to violent material, and makes frequent references to "snuff" movies, as if *this* were what men really liked.

No one has ever been able to find one of these legendary "snuff" films (where women actually are killed for the camera to make commercial pornography), and you would not find images of women being tortured in any porn shop in America, despite the fact that violence is not censored. What MacKinnon is really saying is that male sexual arousal is *about* violence toward women.

And where have we heard that before? In precisely the same places where we heard that women belong in the home, and that women are put on this earth by God to make babies and satisfy men's needs. These same authorities told us that women must be satisfied by bearing children and caring for their families and that women are the sexual and physical chattel of their fathers and husbands.

Antipornography "feminists" centralize pornography in their attempts to address sexism and sexual violence, and as a result go off into foolish blind alleys that take them far from any feminist approach to society. Other feminists look to sex offenders themselves when trying to address sexual violence and discover that these people are not liberals with "sixties morality," but more often men with strongly traditional, repressive values. When Marcia Pally interviewed one of the leading abuse specialists in the United States, she learned that child abusers were very likely to hold strong antipornography attitudes (as shown in her book *Sex & Sensibility*). A real danger exists that antiporn ideology actually promotes the attitudes that lead to sexual violence.

Pornography and Sex Roles

Right-wing moralists very possibly are correct in their view that pornography encourages people to question sex roles. If one were inclined to look at easy correlations, it would not be hard to draw conclusions, as they have, about the prevalence of sexually explicit media in society and the improvement in women's social conditions during the same period. Without a doubt, whatever forces motivated increasing freedom to create and acquire pornography also played a vital role in freeing women from a sexual repression so restrictive that we were seen as "deserving" rape if we showed the slightest interest in something other than home and family.

The society that banned pornography stamped "illegitimate" on birth certificates; in Britain, women who either had been raped or had had consensual sex before marriage were permanently incarcerated in mental hospitals. In the Middle East, pornography is banned, and women's rights are considered an offense to Allah. In China, pornography is a capital offense, and women are forced to abort any pregnancy after the birth of a living child; female infanticide is, of course, rife.

In Britain and America, pornography was decriminalized and

so was abortion; many states in the United States criminalized marital rape, and the United Kingdom also decriminalized homosexuality and eliminated the death penalty. In Western Europe, pornography was decriminalized, sex education became almost universal, teenage pregnancy rates went down, and women are better off compared with men than they are anywhere else in the world. Larry Baron's 1990 research found that areas with high pornography circulation had higher gender equality; he said that the best indicator for low gender equality in a region was the prevalence of religious fundamentalists.

And antiporn women want to tell us that pornography is women's greatest enemy? Then it is time for them to think again. Gender inequality and sexual violence have roots that go far beyond the invention of the printing press and the camera, and we will not eliminate these problems of sexism by duplicating the errors of previous generations who thought they could make society perfect by suppressing sex and stereotyping us all.

But antiporn women have accomplished one important feat on our behalf: they have reminded us that sexually explicit media, in the end, have a relationship with political awareness, and thus must be recognized as protected speech under the First Amendment.

6

"Anti-pornography feminists are part of a human rights movement that seeks to have women's human rights recognized on a global level."

Anti-Pornography Feminists Do Not Harm the Women's Movement

Ann Simonton

Feminists who favor censoring pornography are often criticized by other feminists who oppose censorship. In the following viewpoint, Ann Simonton defends anti-pornography feminists. She argues that pornography harms women and that anyone who supports human rights should advocate the regulation of pornography. Simonton is a contributor to *Z Magazine*, a monthly periodical of left-wing political and social opinion.

As you read, consider the following questions:

1. What five criticisms of the anti-pornography feminists' stance does the author dispute?
2. On what basis does Simonton criticize anti-censorship groups?
3. How does the author refute the argument that anti-pornography feminists are "anti-sex"?

Ann Simonton, "Slandering Antipornography Feminists," *Z Magazine*, March 1994. Reprinted by permission.

Every media pundit from the left, right and middle along with so-called "anti-censorship" groups loves to slander anti-pornography feminists. These attacks, based on lies and distortions, have been repeated so often they have become media "facts." In their standard refrain they claim that: (1) we are aligned with right-wing conservatives; (2) we are a movement comprised of two members: legal theorist Catharine MacKinnon and writer Andrea Dworkin; (3) we advocate censorship; (4) we are all anti-sex; (5) we support "dangerous" legislation that hurts feminists, gays, and lesbians.

Anti-pornography feminists have never aligned themselves with the right's agenda. Right-wing conservatives want women home and pregnant while the male left wants women flat on their backs with their legs spread. Neither agenda appeals to anti-pornography feminists, who work for an end to sexual and racial inequality and white male supremacy.

A Determined Movement

The media loves to reduce us to a movement of two people. Andrea Dworkin and Catharine MacKinnon are, for many of us, the celebrated leaders of this movement because of their years of brilliant theoretical and political work. Pro-pornographers assume that by dragging these women's lives and works through unheard-of media smut, somehow we will all go away. In reality, the anti-pornography movement is a determined movement of millions of women and men nationally and internationally who are working on every level possible to help the public understand the consequences of our culture's addiction to pornographic images and to expose the fact that real people are being hurt through the making and distribution of pornography. Pornography, for many of us, is a form of hate propaganda designed to keep women subordinate to men; it is also a system of sexual exploitation for profit that targets women for rape, battery, and harassment.

A primary frustration for anti-pornography feminists is the difficulty of trying to get people to acknowledge the harm done to women, children, and men through the pornography industry. The majority of women who appear in pornography are also prostitutes and have been sexually abused as children. They are poor and 90 percent would leave the business if they could. Pornography is also controlled by organized crime where force and violence are standard business practice. In a setting like this it is impossible to know if the majority of these women are freely choosing to be photographed and pimped.

Anti-pornography feminists are part of a human rights movement that seeks to have women's human rights recognized on a global level. We want the abuse of women that is condoned through social custom and legal jurisdiction to be seen as the political terrorism it is. Horrifying numbers of women are being beaten, raped, murdered, tortured, abused, and kidnapped. The numbers are not dropping. Our society's denial of what should represent a public health emergency is an affront to women's human rights and serves to protect the pornographers.

Distorting the Meaning of Censorship

Anti-pornography feminists are more staunchly anti-censorship than those who seek to silence them. Apologists for the porn industry who scream about censors have distorted the meaning of censorship and silenced any real debate. Meanwhile, the real issue of stopping violence against women fades into non-existence. We do not believe that pornographers and pimps should have more free speech than the women they profit from using. "Free" speech, in our capitalistic economy, belongs to an elite few who can afford access to it. "Anti-censorship" groups never give the microphone to the women with little access to free speech who, for example, live on the streets being prostituted. Who has done this? In a 1992 BBC documentary Andrea Dworkin insisted that prostitutes—not the media's "Pretty Woman" type—be given a chance to speak. Most of Dworkin's new work remains unpublished in the U.S. The press (*New York Times, Village Voice*) consistently refuse to run corrections to the hundreds of false allegations made about her and her work that vilify her personally.

Groups like the National Coalition Against Censorship, Feminists for Free Expression, and the American Civil Liberties Union (ACLU) have become mouthpieces for pornographers. It is no coincidence that the treasurer for Feminists for Free Expression, Lavada Blanton, works for *Penthouse*. Feminists for Free Expression's board member Marcia Pally is *Penthouse*'s film critic and Feminists for Free Expression receives grants from *Penthouse* and *Playboy*. This same group recently wrote an amicus brief outlining men's right to keep pornography in the workplace. A group called the Media Coalition, whose expressed goal is to protect "sexually explicit materials," hired a PR firm, Gray & Company, to discredit the findings of the Attorney General's Commission on Pornography and any anti-pornography groups or individuals. Their highly successful PR campaign—with three times the budget of the whole Attorney General's Commission—was funded by *Playboy* and *Penthouse* among others.

The ACLU has a long history of taking *Playboy*'s money and also takes a handout from *Penthouse*. They refuse to champion the free speech and civil liberties of anti-pornography feminists—in fact Dworkin and MacKinnon were chosen as ACLU's Censors of the Year (1992).

179

The National Coalition Against Censorship (NCAC) is also partially funded by *Playboy* and *Penthouse*. Their executive director, Leanne Katz, uses their newsletter op-ed pieces to fuel hostile personal attacks on the work and lives of Dworkin and MacKinnon.

The Anti-Sex Label

Anti-pornography feminists are all labeled anti-sex Victorians. We are—according to NCAC's director, Leanne Katz—determined to police every aspect of sexual expression by or about women. This extraordinary statement is a good example of patriarchal reversal: her pornography backers have policed women's sexual expression, creating a climate of scorn for women who won't imitate their standard of beauty, since the 1950s. It is journalistically in vogue to coin new hate-terms for MacKinnon. Laura Flanders (Fairness and Accuracy in Reporting [FAIR])—in her rebuttal of the *Nation's* book review where the reviewer, Carlin Romano, fantasizes raping the author (MacKinnon)—makes certain that readers know she is "no friend of MacKinnon's fetishistic fundamentalism." (FAIR refused to publish a transcript of a speech MacKinnon gave on "political correctness" because their board was divided on the pornography question. So much for Fairness and Accuracy in Reporting.) *Playboy* calls for a knee-jerk hysterical response by saying we are a movement of Nazis. (Camille Paglia takes it further, by labeling all women who don't like *Sports Illustrated's* swimsuit issue as "Stalinists.")

That most anti-pornography feminists don't like what is reflected in mainstream porno flicks and magazines is being construed to mean we are anti-sex. Many of us envision a world where sexual information and imagery would be free of sexism, racism, and homophobia. The celebratory and spiritual aspects of lovemaking have all but been erased in a culture where sex is defined by pornographers who hawk an increasingly narrow and violent version of male sexual fantasy.

The myth that we are all prudes has been permanently tattooed on us by the media's rewriting of Dworkin and MacKinnon's analysis of sexual violence. According to these media hysterics both women believe every act of heterosexual sex is rape and all sex is forced. Neither woman is ever actually quoted as saying this because they have never said it. Critiquing the status of human sexual relations is never easy in a world of gender inequality where such enormous financial interest is vested in keeping women subordinate. The media's outrage is curiously similar to white plantation owners in the antebellum South furious that anyone might dare suggest their slaves were anything but perfectly content.

Many of us have diverse—and even conflicting—ideas about educational and legislative reforms that might begin to curb the flood of pornographic images in our culture. Yet many believe that the enactment of the civil human rights law—developed by Dworkin and MacKinnon—that would allow women and men to sue those that have harmed them is both innovative and promising. Unlike a criminal law where police could come in and grab their version of "obscenity," this civil rights law puts the burden of proof of harm on the plaintiff. Only after the arduous process to prove injury would the pornographers have to pay for the harms they have caused. The enactment of this ordinance, along with educational campaigns to re-sensitize our culture concerning the effects of media images, could mean that media producers and advertisers would no longer have to sell programs, cars, and beer using the pornographer's rules. . . .

The Many Victims of Pornography

There is no such thing as a "victimless" crime. In every crime there is a seller or seducer, and the person who purchases, or the seduced. That person is the immediate victim, and society is the ultimate victim, for with each seduction the moral fabric of society is diminished.

National Coalition Against Pornography, *Information and Resources for Concerned Citizens*, 1995.

NCAC director Katz's accusations that the *Butler* decision is responsible for Canadian Custom's discriminatory seizures is spreading quickly. In February 1992 the Canadian Supreme Court unanimously joined in a new interpretation of obscenity law that defined pornography from a feminist point of view. According to *Butler*, material that shows sex with actual violence, uses children, or is degrading and dehumanizing to women (i.e., that shows women enjoying pain, humiliation, cruel and violent bondage, or sexualized racism) is to be considered harmful to women's safety and equality. *Butler* allows for explicit sex and offers generous protection to any artistic expression.

Immediately after *Butler*, Toronto police raided a gay bookstore, seized the lesbian S/M magazine *Bad Attitude* (that has a Canadian circulation of 40) charged it in court under *Butler* because it contained sex between a young girl and a nurse-caretaker. Canadian Customs officers admit they don't understand the new harms-based definition of porn embodied in *Butler*. The police and the Canadian Customs have an inexcusable history of using discriminatory practices against gay and lesbian bookstores well before *Butler*. According to MacKinnon, who helped argue *Butler* to the Court, "In legal fact, it was easier to use Canada's obscenity law oppressively, including against gay and lesbian materials, before *Butler* than after it. Under *Butler* it is illegal for Customs to seize materials because they are gay or lesbian. Under prior Canadian law, it was legal."

Women Viewed as Expendable

In a discussion against gun control, it would be bizarre not to mention the harm guns do to people. Yet, when anyone suggests controlling pornography and documents the harm done to people, the "censor" label is used to gag further discussion. Any consumer product that was proven as harmful as pornography would never win widespread support.

The underlying problem continues to be the fact that women's lives are cheap and expendable. When prostitutes are killed the numbers have to be in the double digits for an official investigation to take place. Pornography and other property rights take precedence over women's lives and women's safety. Pornography is deemed more important than the women who are trampled in the wake of this 10 billion dollar a year industry.

Exposing the lies that pornography spreads about women will never win popularity contests. It is our challenge to summon the courage to continue the fight for women's dignity and integrity in a society where bigotry and contempt for women is celebrated daily.

Periodical Bibliography

The following articles have been selected to supplement the diverse views presented in this chapter. Addresses are provided for periodicals not indexed in the *Readers' Guide to Periodical Literature*, the *Alternative Press Index*, or the *Social Sciences Index*.

Christian Social Action	"The Manila Declaration on Pornography," June 1995.
Andrea Dworkin et al.	"Pornography and the New Puritans: Letters from Andrea Dworkin and Others," *New York Times Book Review*, May 3, 1992.
Laura Fraser	"A Critic Looks at Pornography from the Inside," *EXTRA!* July/August 1993.
Joanne Furio	"Does Women's Equality Depend on What We Do About Pornography?" *Ms.*, January/February 1995.
Ursula K. Le Guin	"Pornography + Responsibility," *Civil Liberties*, Fall 1993.
Ellen Levy	"She Just Doesn't Understand: The Feminist Face-off on Pornography Legislation," *On the Issues*, Fall 1993.
David McCabe	"The Politics of Porn: Not-So-Strange Bedfellows," *In These Times*, March 7, 1994.
Ms.	"Where Do We Stand on Pornography?" January/February 1994.
Off Our Backs	"Speech, Equality, and Harm," April 1993.
Diana E.H. Russell	"Nadine Strossen: The Pornography Industry's Wet Dream," *On the Issues*, Summer 1995.
Chi Chi Sileo	"Pornographobia: Feminists Go to War," *Insight*, February 27, 1995. Available from 3600 New York Ave. NE, Washington, DC 20002.
Nadine Strossen	"Big Sister Is Watching You," *Advocate*, November 14, 1995.
Sallie Tisdale	"Talk Dirty to Me: A Woman's Taste for Pornography," *Utne Reader*, July/August 1993.
Margaret Wertheim	"The Electronic Orgasm," *Glamour*, March 1995.

For Further Discussion

Chapter 1

1. How does Wendy McElroy distinguish her pro-pornography views from those of Nadine Strossen? Which author's stance on the issue is the most persuasive, and why?

2. Cite some of the evidence that Rosaline Bush, Donna Rice Hughes, John McMickle, and Mark Nichols give to support their view that pornography is harmful. Do you find their evidence persuasive? If so, why? If not, what evidence given by Nadine Strossen, Wendy McElroy, and Leora Tanenbaum do you find convincing?

3. After reading the viewpoints by Linda Marchiano and Leora Tanenbaum, consider this question: Do those who participate in pornography freely choose to do so? Do you believe that these people need protection from pornographers, or should they be left alone to make their own decisions?

Chapter 2

1. Describe how the various authors in this chapter use and/or define the word "censorship". Do any authors avoid using this word? Why is this word used so carefully? If you were to write an editorial advocating the censorship of pornography, would you use the word "censorship" in the article? Why or why not?

2. Some people fear that if government restricts a civil right such as free speech, a "slippery slope" effect will occur in which the right will eventually be completely taken away. Which authors in this chapter express this view as it applies to the censorship of pornography? Are their arguments persuasive? Why or why not?

3. Nina Burleigh believes that pornography should be censored because it harms women. Nadine Strossen believes that this view harms women because it assumes that they are weak and need to be protected. Which view do you find more compelling? Why?

Chapter 3

1. Some experts argue that the Internet is a unique form of communication and as such should not be regulated as extensively as other, more traditional forms of communication.

Based on the viewpoints in this chapter, do you agree with this view? Why or why not?

2. The 1996 Telecommunications Act bars using the Internet to make indecent material available to minors. It requires online services to make good-faith efforts to keep minors away from indecent material. Do you consider this to be a sensible law or a case of excessive censorship? Support your answer with references to the viewpoints.

3. Because they are the people most directly responsible for their children, many experts think that parents—not the government or businesses—should be the ones to regulate children's access to the Internet. Do you agree? Why or why not? How great a portion of the responsibility belongs to parents? to government? to Internet providers?

Chapter 4

1. Robert Jensen and Ann Simonton argue that because pornography harms women, anti-pornography feminists are correct to oppose its production and distribution. What harms do they attribute to pornography? Lynne Segal and Avedon Carol contend that by focusing on pornography, anti-pornography feminists overlook the actual problems facing women. What problems do they cite? Which view do you find more convincing, and why?

2. Lisa Palac went from being an anti-pornography feminist to being the editor of a porn magazine for women. Does her description of her change of opinion affect your view on how pornography affects women? Why or why not?

3. Prior to reading this chapter, what did you assume would be the feminist stance on pornography? Did the chapter change your understanding of the feminist viewpoint? Explain your response.

4. Do you think feminism is a necessary movement today? Why or why not? If you think it is necessary, what do you believe should be the goals of the movement? Does the anti-pornography movement help or hurt the advancement of these goals? Explain your answer.

Organizations to Contact

The editors have compiled the following list of organizations concerned with the issues debated in this book. The descriptions are derived from materials provided by the organizations. All have publications or information available for interested readers. The list was compiled on the date of publication of the present volume; names, addresses, and phone and fax numbers may change. Be aware that many organizations take several weeks or longer to respond to inquiries, so allow as much time as possible.

Adult Video Association
270 N. Canon Dr., Suite 1370
Beverly Hills, CA 90210
(213) 650-7121

The association believes adults should be able to watch what they choose in the privacy of their own homes. It challenges the constitutionality of laws affecting adult videos. The association provides legal information and referrals, lobbies government agencies, maintains a speakers bureau, and conducts educational programs. It publishes a periodic newsletter.

American Civil Liberties Union (ACLU)
132 W. 43rd St.
New York, NY 10036
(212) 944-9800

The ACLU champions the human rights set forth in the U.S. Constitution. It works to protect the rights of all Americans and to promote equality for women, minorities, and the poor. The ACLU opposes censorship and believes that other measures should be used to combat the harms of pornography. The organization publishes a variety of handbooks, pamphlets, reports, and newsletters, including the quarterly *Civil Liberties* and the monthly *Civil Liberties Alert*.

Canadian Civil Liberties Association
229 Yonge St., Suite 403
Toronto, ON M5B 1N9
CANADA
(416) 363-0321
fax: (416) 861-1291

The association works to protect Canadians' civil liberties and to educate the public concerning civil liberties. It opposes censorship of pornography. Among the association's many publications are the books *When Freedoms Collide: The Case for Our Civil Liberties* and *Uncivil Obedience* and the monthly *CCLA News Notes*.

Citizens Against Pornography (CAP)

PO Box 220190
Chantilly, VA 22022-0190
(703) 437-7863

CAP fights the proliferation and sale of magazines such as *Penthouse* and *Playboy* at retail outlets. It also seeks to stop the production and distribution of adult videos and the opening of adult bookstores. CAP provides information to anyone interested in combating pornography. The organization publishes *Update Letter* periodically.

Citizens for Decency Through Law

11000 Scottsdale Rd., Suite 210
Scottsdale, AZ 85254
(602) 483-8787

Citizens for Decency Through Law is one of the oldest anti-pornography groups in the nation. It lobbies for the enforcement of obscenity laws and works to educate the public on the harms of pornography. The organization provides educational materials on pornography.

Citizens for Media Responsibility Without Law

PO Box 2085
Rancho Cordova, CA 95741-2085
(408) 427-2858

Citizens for Media Responsibility Without Law opposes violent pornography. Rather than advocating censorship, however, it believes that the media should take responsibility for not producing or selling violent images. The organization also encourages civil disobedience as an effective way to stop the proliferation of pornography without resorting to censorship. It publishes leaflets and position papers.

Concerned Women for America (CWA)

370 L'Enfant Promenade SW, Suite 800
Washington, DC 20024
(800) 323-2200

CWA's purpose is to preserve, protect, and promote traditional Judeo-Christian values through education, legislative action, and other activities. It believes that pornography harms all of society and should be censored. CWA publishes the monthly *Family Voice* in addition to brochures, booklets, and manuals on numerous issues, including pornography.

Family Research Council

700 13th St. NW, Suite 500
Washington, DC 20005
(202) 393-2100
fax: (202) 393-2134

The council seeks to promote and protect the interests of the traditional family. It opposes pornography as harmful to children and families.

The council publishes the monthly newsletter *Washington Watch* in addition to policy papers on a variety of political and social issues.

Feminists Fighting Pornography
Box 6731, Yorkville Station
New York, NY 10128
(212) 410-5182

Feminists Fighting Pornography lobbies Congress to pass laws regulating pornography. It maintains a speakers bureau and conducts audiovisual presentations. The organization publishes the annual magazine *Backlash Times*.

Free Speech Coalition
22968 Victory Blvd., Suite 248
Woodland Hills, CA 91367
(818) 348-9373
(800) 845-8503

The coalition is the trade association of the adult entertainment and products industry. Members of the coalition believe censoring pornography violates the right of Americans to free speech. The coalition publishes pro-pornography, anti-censorship materials and a sourcebook on the pornography prosecutions and laws throughout the United States.

Morality in Media (MIM)
475 Riverside Dr.
New York, NY 10115
(212) 870-3222

MIM is a national, interfaith organization working to stop illegal trafficking in hardcore pornography through the rigorous enforcement of state and federal obscenity laws. It works to alert and inform the public and government officials about the destructive effects of pornography. MIM has a National Obscenity Law Center, which is a clearinghouse of legal information on obscenity cases. While the group opposes censorship, it believes that obscenity laws should be strictly enforced and that hardcore pornography is not a protected form of speech. It publishes a bimonthly newsletter in addition to educational materials such as *Pornography Has Consequences* and the handbook *TV: The World's Greatest Mind-Bender*.

National Campaign for Freedom of Expression
1402 Third Ave., No. 421
Seattle, WA 98101
(206) 340-9301

The National Campaign for Freedom of Expression is a group of artists, art organizations, and other individuals concerned with fighting censorship of the visual and performance arts. It believes that individuals have a right to determine for themselves what they want to see. The organization offers technical assistance and training to local activists, monitors legislation, provides legal assistance, distributes press releases, conducts educational programs, and maintains a speakers bureau. Its library contains reference clippings and periodicals, and it publishes the quarterly *NCFE Bulletin* and a newsletter.

National Coalition Against Censorship (NCAC)
275 Seventh Ave.
New York, NY 10001
(212) 807-NCAC
fax: (212) 807-6245

NCAC's goal is to fight censorship, including the censorship of pornography. It fights censorship through conferences, educational programs, and community activism. The coalition publishes the newsletter *Censorship News* and educational materials such as *The Sex Panic: Women, Censorship, and "Pornography."*

National Coalition for the Protection of Children & Families
800 Compton Rd. Suite 9224
Cincinnati, OH 45231-9964
(513) 521-6227
fax: (513) 521-6337

The coalition, formerly called the National Coalition Against Pornography, was formed in 1983 to help stop the harm caused by obscenity and child pornography. It is an alliance of citizens and civic, business, religious, health care, and educational groups working to eliminate child pornography and to remove illegal pornography from the marketplace. The coalition lobbies legislatures and educates the public and law enforcement officials on the dangers of pornography. Its National Law Center for Children and Families is a clearinghouse for legal information on child exploitation and illegal pornography. The coalition publishes brochures such as *Children, Pornography, and Cyberspace.*

National Federation for Decency
PO Drawer 2440
Tupelo, MS 38803
(601) 844-5036

The federation works to improve the morality of America. It opposes pornography and advocates the censorship of all pornographic materials. The federation sponsors decency campaigns and publishes a newsletter.

Women Against Pornography
321 W. 47th St.
New York, NY 10036
(212) 307-5055

Women Against Pornography is a national organization that educates the public about the harm pornography does to the safety and status of all women. It conducts tours of New York City's Times Square, to demonstrate that pornography is readily available. Women Against Pornography works with other organizations to lobby legislatures to censor pornography and publishes educational information on the harms of pornography.

Women's Action Alliance
370 Lexington Ave., Suite 603
New York, NY 10017
(212) 532-8330
fax: (212) 779-2846

The alliance was established in 1971 as a national nonprofit service organization that provides educational services and programs to help women become self-sufficient and independent. It publishes educational materials on pornography and *Women in Action*, a quarterly newsletter.

Bibliography of Books

Robert M. Baird and Stuart E. Rosenbaum
Pornography: Private Right or Public Menace? Buffalo: Prometheus Books, 1991.

Alida Brill
Nobody's Business: Paradoxes of Privacy. Reading, MA: Addison-Wesley, 1990.

Avedon Carol
Nudes, Prudes, and Attitudes: Pornography and Censorship. Cheltenham, UK: New Clarion Press, 1994.

Avedon Carol and Alison Assister, eds.
Bad Girls and Dirty Pictures: The Challenge to Reclaim Feminism. London: Pluto Press, 1993.

F.M. Christensen
Pornography: The Other Side. Westport, CT: Praeger, 1990.

David Copp and Susan Wendell, eds.
Pornography and Censorship. Buffalo: Prometheus Books, 1982.

Edward De Grazia
Girls Lean Back Everywhere: The Law of Obscenity and the Assault on Genius. New York:Vintage Books, 1993.

John Drakeford and Jack Hamm
Pornography: The Sexual Mirage. Nashville: Thomas Nelson, 1973.

Andrea Dworkin
Pornography: Men Possessing Women. New York: Dutton, 1991.

Susan M. Easton
The Problem of Pornography: Regulation and the Right to Free Speech. New York: Routledge, 1994.

Neil Gallagher
How to Stop the Porno Plague. Minneapolis: Bethany House, 1977.

Pamela Church Gibson and Roma Gibson, eds.
Dirty Looks: Women, Pornography, Power. Bloomington: Indiana University Press, 1993.

Carol Gorman
Pornography. Chicago: Franklin Watts, 1988.

Susan Griffin
Pornography and Silence: Culture's Revenge Against Nature. New York: Harper and Row, 1981.

Susan Gubar and Joan Hoff, eds.
For Adult Users Only: The Dilemma of Violent Pornography. Bloomington: Indiana University Press, 1989.

Gordon J. Hawkins and Franklin E. Zimring
Pornography in a Free Society. New York: Cambridge University Press, 1991.

Helen Hazen   *Endless Rapture: Rape, Romance, and the Female Imagination.* New York: Scribner, 1983.

Jan Hunter, David   *On Pornography: Literature, Sexuality, and Obscenity Law.* New York: St. Martin's Press, 1993.
Saunders, and Dugald
Williamson, eds.

Catherine Itzin   *Pornography: Women, Violence, and Civil Liberties, a Radical View.* Oxford: Oxford University Press, 1993.

Laura Lederer and   *The Price We Pay: The Case Against Racist Speech, Hate Propaganda, and Pornography.* New York: Hill and Wang, 1995.
Richard Delgado, eds.

Dorchen Leidholdt   *The Sexual Liberals and the Attack on Feminism.* Tarrytown, NY: Pergamon Press, 1990.
and Janice G.
Raymond, eds.

Daniel Linz and   *Pornography.* Newbury Park, CA: Sage, 1993.
Neil Malamuth

Catharine MacKinnon   *Only Words.* Cambridge, MA: Harvard University Press, 1993.

Neil Malamuth and   *Pornography and Sexual Aggression.* Chicago: Ed-Academy Press, 1984.
ward Donnerstein

Wendy McElroy   *XXX: A Woman's Right to Pornography.* New York: St. Martin's Press, 1995.

Susan S. Nash   *Pornography.* Mentor, OH: Generator Press, 1992.

Shirley O'Brien   *Child Pornography.* Dubuque, IA: Kendall/Hunt, 1983.

Franklin Mark   *Sourcebook on Pornography.* New York: Lexington Books, 1989.
Osanka and Sara Lee

Johann, eds.

Marcia Pally   *Sex and Sensibility: The Vanity of Bonfires.* Hopewell, NJ: Ecco Press, 1994.

Robert S. Randall   *Freedom and Taboo: Pornography and the Politics of a Self Divided.* Berkeley and Los Angeles: University of California Press, 1989.

Robert D. Reed and   *Pornography: How and Where to Find Facts and Get Help.* Saratoga, CA: R & E Publishers, 1993.
Danek S. Kaus

Judith A. Reisman   *"Soft Porn" Plays Hardball: Its Tragic Effects on Women, Children, and the Family.* Lafayette, LA: Huntington House, 1991.

Martin Rimm	*Pornographer's Handbook: How to Exploit Women, Dupe Men, and Make Lots of Money.* Pittsburgh: Carnegie Mellon University Press, 1995.
Ray C. Rist, ed.	*Pornography Controversy: Changing Moral Standards in American Life.* New Brunswick, NJ: Transaction, 1974.
Joanna Russ	*Magic Mommas, Trembling Sisters, Puritans, and Perverts: Feminist Essays.* Freedom, CA: Crossing Press, 1985.
Phyllis Schlafly, ed.	*Pornography's Victims.* Alton, IL: Pere Marquette Press, 1987.
Lynne Segal and Mary McIntosh, eds.	*Sex Exposed: Sexuality and the Pornography Debate.* New Brunswick, NJ: Rutgers University Press, 1993.
H. Robert Showers and Barbara Hattemer	*Don't Touch That Dial: The Impact of Media on Children and the Family.* Lafayette, LA: Huntington House, 1992.
Rodney A. Smolla	*Jerry Falwell v. Larry Flynt: The First Amendment on Trial.* Champaign: University of Illinois Press, 1990.
Alan Soble	*Pornography: Marxism, Feminism, and the Future of Sexuality.* New Haven, CT: Yale University Press, 1986.
Adele M. Stan, ed.	*Debating Sexual Correctness: Pornography, Sexual Harassment, Date Rape, and the Politics of Sexual Equality.* New York: Delta Books, 1995.
Robert J. Stoller	*Porn: Myths for the Twentieth Century.* New Haven, CT: Yale University Press, 1991.
John Stoltenberg	*The End of Manhood: A Book for Men of Conscience.* New York: NAL-Dutton, 1993.
John Stoltenberg	*Refusing to Be a Man: Essays on Sex and Justice.* New York: NAL-Dutton, 1990.
John Stoltenberg	*What Makes Pornography "Sexy"?* Minneapolis: Milkweed Editions, 1994.
Nadine Strossen	*Defending Pornography: Free Speech, Sex, and the Fight for Women's Rights.* New York: Scribner, 1995.
U.S. Attorney General	*Final Report of the Attorney General's Commission on Pornography.* Nashville: Rutledge Hill Press, 1986.

Marianna Valverde   *Sex, Power, and Pleasure.* Philadelphia: New So-
                     ciety Publishers, 1987.

Donald Wildmon   *The Case Against Pornography.* Wheaton, IL: Vic-
                     tor Books, 1986.

Linda Williams   *Hard Core: Power, Pleasure, and the "Frenzy of the
                     Visible."* Berkeley and Los Angeles: University
                     of California Press, 1991.

Index

199

154-55, 159-63
as expendable, 182
exploitation of,
  is preceded by pornography,
    151-52
  pornography as, 92
and liberation of sexuality,
  99-101
as objects, 145-46
and pornography, 61, 166,
  173-74
  harm of difficult to prove,
    75-76
  and power, 155-56
  and sex roles, 175-76

subordination of, 100-101
were made for sex, 143
see also feminists
Women Against Pornography,
  166
Women Hating (Dworkin), 102
Women Hurt in Systems of
  Prostitution or Engaged in
  Revolt (WHISPER), 160
Women's Refuge, 152
World Wide Web sites, 118,
  120

Zillmann, Dolf, 46, 172